UNIVERSAL TYPING for Schools

Edith Mackay

BA(Hons) FRSA

Pitman

PITMAN PUBLISHING LIMITED
128 Long Acre, London WC2E 9AN

Associated Companies
Pitman Publishing Pty Ltd, Melbourne
Pitman Publishing New Zealand Ltd, Wellington

First published in Great Britain 1985

British Library Cataloguing in Publication Data
Mackay, Edith
Universal typing for schools.
1. Typewriting
I. Title
652.3   Z49

Printed and bound in Italy by New Interlitho, Milan.

ISBN 0 273 02328 4

Introduction

Typewriting has assumed a new dimension in our technological age. Never has there been such a demand for keyboard operators and secretaries. And new applications of the QWERTY keyboard are appearing in ever more sophisticated forms of office equipment. Basic to the operation of all these is the keyboard skill of touch typing.

Universal Typing for Schools will enable students of every age and ability to master typewriting as quickly as possible.

Most students will learn in class with a teacher. However, instructions and explanations are sufficiently detailed and clear for students learning on their own. In the class situation, they reinforce the guidance of the teacher—and can be used to good effect for homework and during sessions when the class may have to work on its own.

Examination coverage

Universal Typing for Schools covers the requirements of all first level examinations (RSA, Pitman, CSE, etc). It provides thorough keyboard training, and practice in all the documents and skills encountered in first examinations and initial office work.

Special features of Universal Typing for Schools

1 Methodical division into technique sections, units of work, and production tasks (with target times).

2 Step-by-step treatment of new material by:

explanation of new work (including model)
copying the model
applying the new skill and knowledge.

3 Thorough instruction in keyboard mastery.

4 Comprehensive range of remedial and keyboard/technique drills (one in each unit).

5 Programme of speed/accuracy development, progressing from one-minute to five-minute timings.

6 Emphasis on the simplest and quickest typewriting methods—consistent with good technique and display.

All these features combine to give maximum help to teachers so they have more time for the major part of their function—guidance to the individual student.

Structure of the course

Universal Typing for Schools is methodically divided into technique sections, units of work and revisionary production tasks. These act and interact upon each other, forming one coherent and interlocking whole.

Technique sections These explain the new typewriting work clearly and concisely: the explanations are related to a typed model which the students copy.

The technique sections are planned so that the new work progresses in a systematic step-by-step manner. The students are expected to assimilate only a little new material at any one time and the new knowledge and techniques are logically built on what they know and can already do. These technique sections also provide conveniently arranged notes for subsequent reference and consolidation.

Units of work In general, these follow a set pattern:

1 A keyboard or technique drill.

2 Mastery and application of the new work set out in the related technique section.

3 Additional typewriting tasks in which the student has to adapt the new knowledge and techniques to fresh material.

4 Speed/accuracy development.

Lessons need not of course follow this pattern. Sometimes, for instance, teachers will want to take speed/accuracy development earlier.

Production tasks Production tasks (each with a target time) are included at intervals throughout the course. They provide revision of work already covered so that the students are never allowed to 'forget' what they have learned.

Supplementary texts

Many teachers will wish to give more practice in the different documents than is possible in this book. This need is met in **Universal Typing Graded Production Tasks—Elementary**, where the topics follow the same order as here, and at the appropriate level.

Additional practice in remedial and keyboard/technique drills may be considered necessary to meet the high levels of speed and accuracy required in today's offices. **Universal Typing Keyboard Speed and Proficiency** provides suitable material.

Teachers will find helpful **Universal Typing Teachers Book**—which provides a wealth of information and material to help lighten the teachers' task and make learning more efficient. It includes a wide range of general notes; learning objectives for each section; teaching notes; letterheads, memo-heads, etc (to copy and distribute) for realism; and a typed key of the typing tasks set.

It is hoped teachers will find that **Universal Typing for Schools**, together with the supplementary texts, will help make teaching typewriting a more successful, and therefore more satisfying, experience.

Passage 8 (5 minutes)   SI 1.38   *Strokes*

People of all ages in all parts of the world have always loved   64
gardens. This was as true of the Greeks and Romans, and other   130
ancient civilizations, as it is of every country in the modern   193
world. Gardening can bring the wonders and beauty of nature   255
to the homes of everyone. Whether in a large or small garden,   319
on a terrace or balcony, or just in a few indoor plant pots,   380
the pleasure of growing things is the same. As part of our   441
daily lives we can all enjoy the cycle of nature from the tiny   504
seed to the full-blown flower, yielding its own new seed to   564
start the process all over again.   599

Indoor gardening is an art in itself. There are flowering   660
house plants and decorative foliage plants for all rooms. As   723
with any living thing, plants need moisture, food and light.   784
Also of course, for good health, these should be in the right   847
amounts. With a little patience and skill, the results can be   911
delightful. Merely growing things, however, has an exciting   973
charm of its own.   990

(198 words)

Passage 9 (5 minutes)   SI 1.38

Stamp collecting is a hobby which gives equal interest and   60
pleasure from youth to old age. For a start, you have   116
portraits and pictures in a wealth of colour, delightful to   176
the eye. Then, as you acquire the stamps of different   232
countries, your knowledge of geography grows - and no less of   294
history, for stamps are used to mark the great events in a   353
nation's past. The best-known authors, painters and composers   417
have their place too. From the realm of nature you will find   480
bird, animal and floral stamps, typical of each country.   537
Technology is covered as well.   569

With the help of an illustrated catalogue you can build up at   632
quite small cost a wide-ranging collection of stamps dating   692
back many years in time. It is true that rare stamps are   751
expensive, some costing as much as thousands of pounds. There   815
is, however, a wealth of choice between the cheapest and   872
dearest stamps. Anyone who puts money into a collection has   934
the knowledge that over the years stamps have proved to be a   995
good investment.   1011

(202 words)

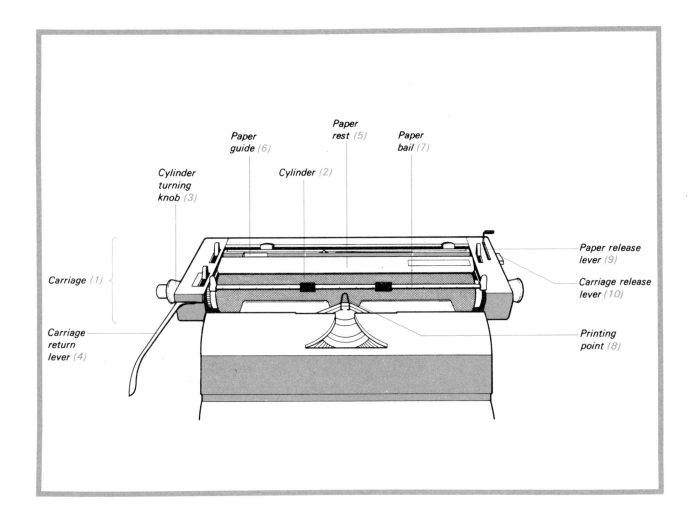

Paper guide (6)   Paper rest (5)   Paper bail (7)

Cylinder turning knob (3)   Cylinder (2)

Paper release lever (9)

Carriage (1)

Carriage release lever (10)

Carriage return lever (4)

Printing point (8)

1 **Carriage** The whole of the top part of the type-writer. It moves the width of a letter each time a key or the space bar is struck. (*If you are using a 'golf-ball' electric typewriter, the carriage remains stationary while the type-ball head moves along the cylinder.*)

2 **Cylinder** (often called the 'platen') The long roller on the carriage, round which the paper turns for typing.

3 **Cylinder turning knobs** These two knobs (one at each end of the cylinder) are turned to move the paper to the required position for typing.

4 **Carriage return lever** The large lever on the left of the carriage, used to return the carriage and turn up the cylinder (and hence the paper) for the start of a new line of typing. *On electric machines this operation is carried out by striking (with the right-hand little finger) a large return key to the right of the keyboard.*

5 **Paper rest** The metal support behind the cylinder, on which the paper rests as it is fed into the type-writer.

6 **Paper guide** An adjustable metal plate that stands out from the left side of the paper rest. The left-hand edge of the paper is aligned with the guide as it is inserted into the typewriter.

7 **Paper bail** A movable rod with rubber grips, in front of the cylinder. The rod holds the paper back against the cylinder. It is marked with a paper scale, which is aligned with the front and back scales on the carriage: all of these measure the width of the paper in terms of the size of type, and are used for display work.

8 **Printing point** This is the point where the letter or character is printed through the ribbon as the key is struck.

9 **Paper release lever** When moved forwards, this lever releases pressure on the paper so that it can be freely moved if inserted crookedly, etc. It should be used when removing paper from the typewriter.

10 **Carriage release levers** Either of these levers (one at each end of the carriage) frees the carriage so that it can be moved quickly from one position to another by hand. While the thumb presses the release lever down, the rest of the hand *must* hold the cylinder knob to control the carriage movement—to prevent damage to the typewriter.

It sometimes happens that an angry person storms into a	57
typist's office waving a sheet of paper and demanding to know	120
why anyone ever typed this. He points out that it makes no	181
sense and insists that he could never have written such	237
rubbish.	247

What has happened is a common pitfall when typing from copy.	309
The typist, not thinking about the sense of what she is typing,	374
and not keeping her eyes on the copy as much as she should, has	438
missed out whole lines. This is a common error, particularly	501
when the same word is repeated on the next line or a little	561
further down. The word is picked up in the wrong place - and	624
typed nonsense results.	649

Of course, such an angry situation would not arise if the typed	714
work was carefully checked before being passed as finished.	774
One has to be particularly alert when typing speed tests - as	837
this kind of mistake is more common than you may think.	892

(178 words)

It is easy to see why jogging is popular. We all know that	62
regular exercise in the fresh air plays a big part in keeping	124
a fit and healthy body. Yet many of us have no aptitude or	185
liking for games, nor have we any chance to play them	239
regularly. The same applies to many other pastimes - like	299
swimming, gymnastics, skating or dancing - and they are not,	360
of course, always possible in the open air.	404

The merit of jogging is that it can be done where people	462
please, at any hour of the day or night, by persons of any	521
age, either alone or in company. A round of the city or	579
suburban house blocks is as good as a cross-country run. The	642
jogger can set his or her own pace, and if necessary drop the	704
trot to a walk till breath is recovered.	746

While the natural loner enjoys jogging alone, many people	805
prefer to go out with friends in groups of joggers formed in	866
offices and neighbourhoods. The choice is entirely their own.	928

(186 words)

Setting margins	Typewriters differ in their means of margin setting. A common device is two movable margin stops at the back of the carriage. (Sometimes, but not very often, these are on the front of the carriage). It is a simple matter to press and slide these stops to the required positions on the paper scale. Other typewriters, where the margin stops are out of sight, are more complicated. They are adjusted in this way: *a* Move the carriage to the point at which the margin is already set. *b* Press a margin key (or lever) and at the same time move the carriage using a carriage release lever. *c* Release the keys when you reach the margin setting required. Consult your typewriter booklet if there is no one to explain it to you.
Paper	Of the different sizes of paper that can be used for typing, the most common is called A4 (210 mm × 297 mm: approx $8\frac{1}{4}$ in × $11\frac{3}{4}$ in). You should use only this size unless told otherwise. Use it with the short side at the top. With good-quality typing paper, there is a correct side for typing on: this is smoother than the reverse side.
Ribbon indicator	This is placed in different positions on different typewriters, and can be recognized by its colour code—red, white and blue (or black). When set at blue, the top half of the ribbon is used for typing; when set at red, the bottom half of the ribbon is used. The white position disconnects the ribbon, for stencil work, etc.
Size of type	There are a number of different sizes and kinds of type. The two most common are called *elite* (or 12-pitch) and *pica* (or 10-pitch). Examples follow.

```
Elite type has 12 characters to the inch (2.5 cm).
Pica type has 10 characters to the inch (2.5 cm).
```

	Because elite is smaller than pica, you can type more letters across the page. This is why the margin settings for elite and pica are different. The left-hand margin setting you will first use is described as elite 35, pica 25. According to whether your typewriter has elite or pica type, you should set your margin at 35 or 25 on the paper scales. This will give the required margin, provided the left-hand edge of the paper is at 0 on the paper scales.
Line space selector	This is a small lever, usually on the left of the carriage, with a 1 2 3 scale. Some machines have intermediary settings as well ($1\frac{1}{2}$, $2\frac{1}{2}$). The line space selector governs the space between the lines of type— as shown in the following examples.

Line space selector at 1   *Line space selector at 2*   *Line space selector at 3*

```
2.5 cm   This is typed in single    In double spacing there   In treble spacing 2
(1 in)   line spacing.  There is        (space)                   (space)
6 lines  no full line of space      is one full line of           (space)
         between the lines of type.     (space)               lines of space are
         But the lines are, of      space between the type.       (space)
         course, clearly separated.                               (space)
                                                               left between the type.
```

Additional space between the lines can be obtained by using the carriage return lever (or key, with electric machines).

People seem to like or dislike crossword puzzles - with quite   63
strong feeling. The crossword lover can scarcely glance at   124
the news headlines before having a shot at the puzzle. To   184
those who do not have such interest, the chequer-board which   245
appears each day on its allotted page is something to be   302
totally ignored.   320

No doubt a liking for crosswords depends to some extent on a   381
measure of success in solving them. This may take some time,   444
as there are conventions and verbal quirks in the setting of   505
crosswords that can only be recognized with practice and by   565
comparing a lot of solutions with the clues. In favour of   625
crosswords it can be said that they make you think about the   686
use of words and help to widen vocabulary.   728

                                                        (146 words)

All of us are familiar with detailed maps of the continents   61
and land masses of the world. We are also aware that maps   121
have been made of the Moon and, more recently, of Mars. It   184
therefore perhaps comes as a surprise to realise that, apart   245
from a few small areas, no detailed maps of the ocean floor   305
exist; knowledge is scanty even of the more shallow   357
continental shelves.   379

Cameras cannot be used for sea-floor mapping because of the   440
lack of light. Thus it is necessary to use techniques that   501
make use of sound waves. A way of scanning the sea bed by   561
means of a narrow sound beam has been successfully used on   620
the deep ocean beds as well as on the easier continental   677
shelves. In this way a picture of the contours can be   733
gradually built up. It is, however, a slow process, and it   794
will be some years before such a mammoth task is completed.   853

                                                        (171 words)

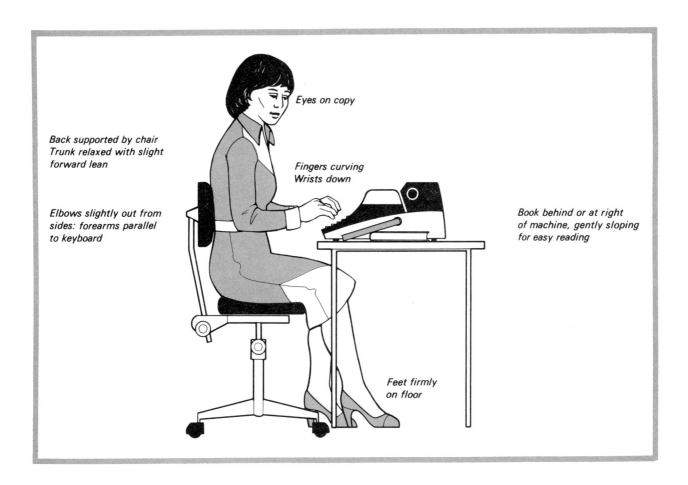

Posture Because you sit for long periods when you type, it is important that you sit correctly. A comfortable, relaxed sitting position will help avoid tiredness, aches and pains—often the cause of typewriting errors and lack of progress.

Chair Use a purpose-designed chair with an upholstered seat. You will be able to adjust its height. Adjust the chair so that your forearms are at the same slope as the keyboard and you do not have to stretch the arms or to crouch.

Arms and wrists Keep your wrists down—yet not so low that they rest on the typewriter frame. When typing, there should be minimum wrist and arm movement, leaving the work to the fingers.

Place the front of your typewriter parallel to and flush with the edge of the desk.

The **book** (the copy) is ideally positioned square in front of the eyes. If this is not possible it is best placed to the right of the typewriter. Here it is on the opposite side (with manual machines) to the carriage return lever: this prevents the hand sweeping between the eyes and the copy each time the carriage is returned. If the habit of always positioning the copy on the right is developed, you can more easily adjust from an electric to a manual typewriter.

Electric typewriters *Note that the keyboard on an electric typewriter is less steep than on a manual machine. Your hands should be held flatter and your fingers should be less curved than for manuals.*

The following passages for speed/accuracy development are for use from Unit 41 onwards. Full instructions are given in Technique Section 16 on pages 84 and 85.

Passage 1 (3 minutes)   *SI 1.38*   *Strokes*

Have you ever made a journey by railway sleeping-car? Have   63
you known the excitement of settling down in a cosy bunk, to   124
the rhythm of the wheels below, and waking up to a new   179
landscape flashing by the carriage windows?   225

For most people, travel by railway sleeper is a thing of the   287
past, and long rail journeys are rare even by day. The car,   348
the coach and the plane have largely taken over. Perhaps   407
already the railway sleeper is just a fading memory.   459

                                                          (92 words)

Passage 2 (3 minutes)   *SI 1.38*

Many typists and secretaries find good jobs abroad, often on   62
contract to a foreign firm for a fixed period of time. Since   125
English is so widely used throughout the world, it is not   184
essential to be able to speak and write a second language   242
though it is a great help. High speeds and standards in   300
office skills are demanded - and met, since competition for   360
good jobs abroad is keen. Many young people enjoy life   417
abroad in this way as it gives them a chance to travel and   476
see places they might not otherwise visit.   518

                                                         (104 words)

Passage 3 (3 minutes)   *SI 1.35*

Proverbs express truths or wise sayings in familiar and   57
often colourful ways. To say that the grass is always   113
greener on the other side means that we always tend to feel   173
our neighbour is more fortunate than we are; and of course   232
he thinks the same about us.   262

The saying that he who hesitates is lost is a warning against   325
not being able to make up our mind. To be told to look   382
before you leap is advice against rashness. Although these   443
may seem to conflict, they are really only saying that there   504
are times for bold decision and times for caution. Proverbs   566
enrich our language and it would be the poorer without them.   626

                                                         (125 words)

The expert typist knows:

The typewriter and its correct operation

The correct sitting position

The correct key-striking action

If *you* want to become an expert, follow this example

Do things *the right way from the start,* for bad habits are hard to break

Try to work out *why* things should be done the way you are told

He received 60 letters: there was only time to answer 45.
The jar contained 123 coins - 78 of them in first-class (or
even mint) condition. Did 24 or 25 come to the party? Ken
ran 8 miles in the sizzling heat!

LONGFELLOW GROUP plc

Half-year ended 30 September 19--

(Single spacing & 1 cc please)

Typist — leave here an unruled space measuring 3 inches (7.5 cm) x 3 inches for addition later of a diagram 2¾ x 2¾.

Sales & Profits The Group continued to achieve a healthy rate of growth in the first 6 months of the current financial yr. Sales increased by 14.3 per cent to £1,087.0m, & at £142.8m the pre-tax profit was 12.1 per cent higher than in the corresponding period last yr.

Interim dividend (last yr's figures in brackets) The directors have ~~decided~~ declared an interim div per ordinary share of 5.1p (4.6p) totalling £36.8m (£33.1m).

Currency exchange rates In accordance w the Group's normal practice at the interim stage, the results of overseas cos for the half-yr have been translated into sterling at the rates of exchange ruling at 31 March, except for the results of cos in Brazil and Mexico wh have been translated into sterling at 30 September rates of exchange. If the rates of exchange at 30 September had been applied to the interim results of all overseas cos, turnover wd have increased by £56.6m and profit before taxation by £7.7m.

27 November 19--

Line space selector Set at 1 for single spacing (no line of space between the lines of type)

Ribbon indicator Set at blue (or black).

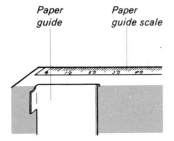

Paper guide   *Paper guide scale*

Paper guide Make sure this is lined up with 0 on the paper scales.

Paper bail Lift this forward and up—away from the cylinder—so that your sheet of typing paper can be smoothly inserted into the typewriter without catching on the paper grips on the paper bail.

Insert paper Use A4 paper. Use a backing sheet behind your typing paper to prevent damage to the cylinder by the type. Hold the double paper level in your left hand, backing sheet towards you. Then carefully slip it between the cylinder and the paper rest, so that the left-hand edge of the paper rests against the raised edge of the paper guide. Turn the right-hand cylinder knob away from you to draw the paper up round the cylinder.

Straighten paper Keep turning the right-hand cylinder knob until you can press the paper back at the left, against the paper guide. If both edges fit evenly against the paper guide, the paper is straight. If the paper is not straight, loosen it by means of the paper release lever: then straighten it and return the paper release lever to its usual position.

Paper grips Return the paper bail against the paper. Check that the paper grips are spaced out to hold the paper evenly against the cylinder (each grip approximately 5 cm (2 in) from the edge of the paper).

Top of paper By turning the right-hand cylinder knob towards you, draw the paper back until the top edge of the sheet is just covered by the paper grips on the paper bail.

Set margins
Left: elite 35, pica 25.
Right: move it out of the way for the present—to the extreme right-hand position.

Check that the carriage is as far as it will go to the right, so that the printing point is at the left margin position for the start of typing.

Check posture and position at the typewriter. As you sit at the typewriter, check all the points on page 3.

You can now begin to type.

John has 2 homes, a town house and a country cottage. His
telephone numbers are 01-969 48735 and 0254 89763.

1 *Technique Sections 24A and 24B (pages 120 and 121)*

When you have really grasped the content of the two passages, type them, each
on a sheet of A4 paper.

2 Type the following letter that contains a main heading and sub-headings. Type
the shoulder headings as shown, with initial capitals and underscoring. Take one
carbon copy. (It is for dispatch today.)

Ref EW. PT. 46903

Mrs B James
20 Mountjoy Avenue
LEEDS LS2 4AX

Dear Mrs James

BUNGALOWS IN THE WOODLANDS AREA

When you telephoned me yesterday you said you were interested
in buying a property in the ~~Southall~~ Woodlands area of this town, preferably
a bungalow with a good-sized garden. The following are attractive
properties in the price range you indicated.

Pentlands, Longridge Drive, Woodlands
@ This is virtually new bung, enjoying open country views over
the Downs. It is soundly built and well appointed. The accommodation consists of lounge, dining-room, 3 bedrooms, bathroom &
✓ kitchen. There is a ~~well-kept~~ garden of 3/4 acre.
Price: £35,000 freehold. Rates: £380 pa.

Fernbank, 42 Queen's Road, Woodlands
One of the older bungalows in the district, in the most favoured
area within easy reach of schools and shops. Accommodation:
lounge/dining-room, 3 bedrooms, study, bathroom & kitchen. Well
stocked garden of 1/2 acre.
Price: £30,000 f/hold. Rates: £300 pa.

I shall be pleased to arrange for you to view these properties
at yr convenience.
Yrs sincerely.
E Willow Office Manager

Look at your typewriter keyboard. Find the home keys (in colour on the above diagram) and curve your fingers over them without actually touching the keys. See that G and H are 'free' in the middle.

When typing, always maintain this central position of the hands at the keyboard and only move away from it to strike another key: the finger should then return immediately to its home key.

Striking the keys

Manuals Strike each key firmly and sharply with the tip of the finger—as though the key were very hot.

Electrics Strike each key with the tip of the finger with a light but sharp tap.

Practise striking the home keys in any order—to get the right action and 'feel'. Now type the following line of home row letters. Keep your eyes on the book as much as possible; concentrate and say each letter to yourself as you type it.

```
ffffaaaajjjj;;;;ffffaaaajjjj;;;;
```
Return the carriage to start a new line

Returning the carriage

Manuals The *carriage return lever* is operated by a quick sweep of the left hand and forearm. The hand should be held flat (with the palm down and fingers closed) and should strike the lever with just enough force to ensure that the carriage reaches the left margin stop. The left hand should move quickly back to its home keys: the right hand does not move from its home keys.

Electrics Quickly strike the *carriage return key* at the right of the keyboard with the little finger of the right hand. Then immediately return it to its home key.

With practice, you should be able to operate the carriage return without looking up.

TYPES OF SUB-HEADING
(Within the Body of the Work)

Shoulder Headings

Shoulder headings are an alternative to paragraph headings as sub-headings within continuous typing. There is one main difference between them. Whereas with paragraph headings the text follows on the same line as the heading, with shoulder headings the text starts on a separate line. This makes shoulder headings stand out better.

SHOULDER HEADINGS

This is an example of a shoulder heading. You will see that it begins at the left-hand margin point, and is followed by one line of space before the text begins. Shoulder headings may be typed with closed capitals, as in this example, and underscored for extra prominence if desired. (With electronic typewriters an alternative is bold type.) There should be no full stop after a shoulder heading.

Other Styles of Shoulder Heading

Shoulder headings can also be typed in initial capitals, with or without underscoring, or using bold type with electronic typewriters.

BLOCKED OR INDENTED PARAGRAPHS

    The shoulder headings above are followed by blocked paragraphs. Indented paragraphs can be used if preferred, as in this example. Note, however, that shoulder headings themselves, unlike paragraph headings, are never indented: they always begin at the left-hand margin.

ENUMERATING SHOULDER HEADINGS

Shoulder headings can be enumerated just like paragraph headings - using either numbers or letters to list them.

1 Method 1

The numbers or letters can be typed at the left-hand margin point, followed by a stop, enclosed in brackets, or merely standing on their own.

2 Method 2

If extra prominence is desired, the letters or numbers can be typed within the left-hand margin. To do this, depress the margin release key and backspace the required number of spaces into the left-hand margin.

CONSISTENCY OF STYLE

Within any single piece of work, consistency of style is important - as in most typing matters. In fact it is one of the features of the expert typist.

Now type these two lines:

```
ddddaaaakkkk;;;;ddddaaaakkkk;;;;
ssssaaaallll;;;;ssssaaaallll;;;;
```

Return carriage
Return carriage twice

Your type should give an even impression. With manual typewriters you must strike the keys with an even touch. There is no problem here with electrics.

Using the space bar

The space bar is the long bar at the bottom of the keyboard. It should be tapped sharply with the thumb. (Most people prefer to use the right-hand thumb, but if you are left-handed you may find using the left thumb easier. Whichever you adopt, *it is best always to use the same thumb.*) Each time you tap the space bar, one space will appear on the paper: keep your fingers over the home keys while you operate it.

Now type this line three times as shown, with one space after each letter. Say each letter to yourself as you type it. And say *space* to yourself each time you tap the space bar.

```
a ; s l d k f j a ; s l d k f j
a ; s l d k f j a ; s l d k f j
a ; s l d k f j a ; s l d k f j
```

Did you remember to:

a keep your fingers over the home keys?
b strike the keys correctly?
c concentrate and say each letter to yourself as you typed it?
d say *space* each time you tapped the space bar?
e leave one space after each character?
f keep your eyes on the book as much as possible?

If all your answers are *yes*, you will start Unit 1 with confidence. This confidence will help you to master the skill of typing quickly. If your answer is *no* to any of these questions, copy the above line of typing again in the correct manner.

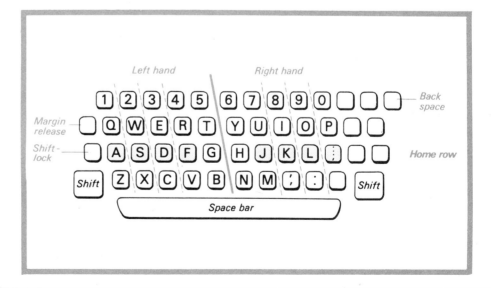

TECHNIQUE 1   Typewriter operation   Practise skills   **7**

TYPES OF SUB-HEADING
(Within the Body of the Work)

Paragraph Headings

Sometimes you will need to type material which has a main heading (and
perhaps sub-headings) at the top - either blocked or centred - and
which also has sub-headings within the body of the work. The latter
can be dealt with in several ways. A common method is to use
paragraph headings.

Paragraph Headings   This is an example of a paragraph heading. You
will see that the text begins on the same line as the heading.
Paragraph headings may be typed in different ways. This one is in
lower case with initial capitals and underscored. In paragraph
headings, underscoring is optional, but the extra prominence it gives
is desirable, particularly where lower case letters are used. (With
electronic typewriters an alternative is bold type.)

Other Styles of Paragraph Heading   Paragraph headings can be typed in
closed capitals, with or without underscoring, or using bold type with
electronic typewriters.

FULL STOP   Whether typed in lower or upper case letters, paragraph
headings may be typed with or without a following full stop. If a full
stop is used, it should be followed by 2 spaces before the text begins.
If, as here, a stop is not used after the paragraph heading, 3 spaces
should be left before starting the text.

    Blocked or Indented Paragraphs   Paragraph headings are often
blocked, beginning at the left-hand margin point, as in the examples
above: this blocked method is the most widely used one. However,
paragraph headings may also be indented, beginning 5 spaces to the
right of the left-hand margin, as in this example.

Enumerating Paragraph Headings   Sometimes you will want to number or
list in some way your paragraph headings. This can be done by using
numbers - 1 2 3 etc, or using letters - a b c etc.

1 Method 1   The numbers or letters are often typed at the left-hand
margin point, followed by a stop, enclosed in brackets, or merely
standing on their own.

2 Method 2   They can also be typed within the left-hand margin, to make
them stand out better. To do this, depress the margin release key and
backspace the required number of spaces into the left-hand margin.

Consistency of Style   Within any single piece of work, consistency of
method in all these matters is important.

General instructions

(for Units 1 to 7)

Paper   Use A4 paper.

Margins
Left: elite 30, pica 20.,
Right: move it out of the way—to the extreme right-hand position.

Left-hand edge of paper at 0 on the paper scales.

Copy each line at least twice. Use single spacing (line space selector at 1) but leave one line of space before proceeding to a different line of copy (by using the carriage return twice).

Mistakes   Type carefully, but if you make a mistake, ignore it and type on. Never overtype by typing the correct letter over the error. Remember, we all make mistakes! Later on you will be told how to correct your work.

Check your typing   Check your typing frequently and draw a circle round each word that contains an error. For extra practice, retype line 1 of the exercise introducing each new key.

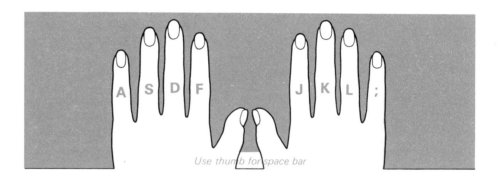

As you type, say each letter to yourself and 'think' the finger you are using. Say 'space' each time you tap the space bar.

Practise home keys

1 asdf ;lkj asdf ;lkj asdf ;lkj asdf ;lkj; Brisk, even strokes

2 ass add aff ;ll ;kk ;jj ass add aff ;ll;

3 fdd fss faa jkk jll j;; fdd fss faa jkkj

4 aff ;jj add ;kk ass ;ll aff ;jj add ;kk;

5 faa j;; fss jll fdd jkk faa j;; fss jllj

Use home keys

6 a jaffa salad; alaska salad; all salads; One space after ; (semi- colon)

7 a lass falls; lads fall; dad falls alas;

8 ask a lad; ask a lass; ask dad; ask all;

UNIT 1   Home keys   **8**

At first, Hazel was extremely awkward skating on ice, but she persevered and conquered a compulsive urge just to give up.

1

Typist — use A4 paper, double spacing for body of table (extra space after Rome)

WINTER HOLIDAY INDEX

From	Holiday Centre	Pages
£95	Tenerife	5 - 12
£90	Gran Canaria	13 - 16
£95	Lanzarote	17 - 19
£86	Malta	20 - 23
£78	Majorca	24 - 26
£80	Algarve	27 - 33
£60	Benidorm	34 - 37
£55	Costa del Sol	38 - 41
£110	Madeira	44 - 45
£95	Tunisia	42 - 43
£300	Barbados	46 - 48
£100	Rhodes	49
£80	Athens and Tel Aviv	50 - 51
£80	Rome	52 - 53
Advance	Charter Flights	54
General	Information	55
Booking	Conditions	56
Holiday	Insurance	57
Booking	Form	58

2

Position centrally on A4 paper. Double spacing for body of table please

FUEL AND POWER CONSUMPTION
(in million tons coal equivalent)

	1963	1973	1983
Coal (net)	201·1	195·5	120·5
Oil	22·2	65·5	157·6
Nuclear Energy	—	0·9	10·5
Natural Gas	—	0·1	36·7
Hydro-power	0·9	1·7	2·0
	224·2	263·7	327·3

Important technique points

Keep the 'central' position of the hands at the keyboard with the fingers over the home keys. Move away from the 'home' position only to strike another key: then return to the home key immediately.

Keep your eyes on the book when you type.

Strike each key sharply.

When you type, move only the finger you are using. Keep wrist and arm movement to a minimum.

Always sit correctly at your typewriter—as illustrated and described on page 3.

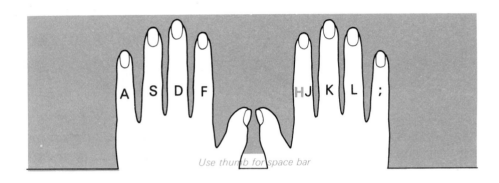

Use thumb for space bar

Revise keys learned

1 ffa jj; ffs jjl ffd jjk ffa jj; ffs jjl;

2 all jaffa salads; all jaffa salads fall;

3 flak falls; as flak falls all dads fall;

New reaches

When learning a new 'reach' always practise the required finger movement, from the home key and back, before actually typing it. Do this first looking at the typewriter, then without looking. Do not start typing a new letter until you can confidently move the home key finger to the new key and back without looking at the machine. *This is most important.*

H

use J finger

4 jjh jjh jjh jhh jhh jhh jhj jhj jhj jhhj

5 a; as; has; a all hall; hall hall shall;

6 a; add; had; as has; has had; hall shall   Sitting correctly?

7 a lass has salad; a lad has had a salad;

8 a lad shall fall; a lass has had a fall;

Use keys learned

9 dad has flasks; lads fall as flak falls;

10 dad has fads; ash falls; dad shall lash;

11 a lass had a jaffa salad; all had salad;

(*Additional material on page 15*)

The boys' choice was between 4 of the grocer's best Cox's apples at 12p each and 2 of the baker's cakes at 24p each. It didn't take them long to go for the apples. For health and enjoyment, wouldn't you have done the same?

1 Type the following table with column headings on A5 landscape paper. With the blocked style of layout, column headings begin at the tab-stop positions.

When deciding on the widest line in the column, the column heading is treated as part of the column. Leave a line of space below column headings. (For revision of footnotes, see page 90.)

REVISED SALARY SCALES*
(for typists + clerk/typists) *2 lines of space*

double spacing →

Grade	Minimum	Maximum
3	£4,800	£5,500
2	£5,750	£6,500
1‡	£6,750	£7,500

* To take effect from 1 Jan 19--.
‡ Must have worked within the Group for at least 6 months.

2 Type the following on A4 paper, using double spacing for the body of the table. Insert leader dots as shown (see page 113.)

TOTAL TURNOVER IN FIRST 2/3 YEARS' TRADING
(including departmental break-down)

	year before last 19-- £	*last year* 19-- £	*This yr* 19-- £
Women's Clothing	100 879	108 964	122 405
Men's Clothing	80 750	82 000	88 688
Furniture	245 760	260 233	278 945
Household Goods	65 123	68 499	72 108
Sports Equipment	45 163	44 281	43 187
Books	56 784	58 174	59 986
TOTAL	£594 459	£622 151	£665 379

3 This year's figures have now been confirmed so please type the above table again, this time showing the first 3 years' trading figures.

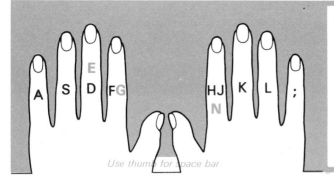

Use thumb for space bar

Reminder Read again the instructions on page 8 and the technique points on page 9. Make sure you follow them.

Finger exercise When you start learning to type, you may find it difficult to move each finger independently of the others. In your spare moments, practise tapping the fingers, in turn, on the table in front of you. This will help strengthen the finger muscles and result in better independent finger action at the typewriter.

Revise keys learned

1   jjh jjh jjh jhh jhh jhh jhj jhj jhj jhhj
2   a lad shall ask a lass; dad has a flask;
3   a lass has a sash; lads had jaffa salad;

E

use D finger

4   dde dde dde dee dee dee ded ded ded deed   One space after ;
5   deed heed ell fell; eel heel ease easel;
6   dales kale sales; jade jaded fade faded;

7   he fell dead; she fell dead; heads fell;
8   he feels sad; she sells eels; she leads;

G

use F finger

9   ffg ffg ffg fgg fgg fgg fgf fgf fgf fggf   Return carriage sharply without looking up
10   fag lag sag jag; edge ledge sedge hedge;
11   a as gas; gaff gall gale; egg legs kegs;

12   a glad lass had eggs; she sells glasses;
13   a gas leak flashed; he has jagged a leg;

N

use J finger

14   jjn jjn jjn jnn jnn jnn jnj jnj jnj jnnj   Strike space bar evenly
15   jeans sane lane need nag send lend fend;
16   ankle knee keen seen hen den lens sense;

17   he needs gas leads; he kneels; send ale;
18   lend dad a hand; send hen feed and sand;

Use keys learned

19   she sells jade and shells; he sells ale;
20   gales lash seas; hedges and lakes flash;
21   a sad lad has a keen head and lean hand;

(*Additional material on page 15*)

Weakness and timidity explain his failure in a legal career. He has great ability, but lacks the confidence to assert himself and achieve success. Gradually he has given way to disappointment and idleness. Perhaps a fresh interest and sense of urgency will be inspired by his new teaching position. It might enable him to redeem the past and enjoy a better future.

1   *Technique Section 23 (pages 113 and 114)*

Following the instructions given, type the table headed *PRECIOUS/SEMI-PRECIOUS STONES*. Use the same method for all your tabulation work. With practice, you will find it easy to follow, and you will soon get to know the method by heart.

2   Type the following three-column table on A5 landscape paper:

WORDS OFTEN MIS-SPELT

accommodate	friend	scarcely
embarrass	occurred	receive
believe	independent	transferred
definite	privilege	separate

3   Type the following four-column tabulation on A5 landscape:

SOME WELL-KNOWN METALS
(in alphabetical order)

aluminium	gold	mercury
chromium	iron	nickel
cobalt	lead	platinum
copper	magnesium	tin

4   Type the following three-column table with figures:

DISTANCES BY ROAD BETWEEN MAJOR TOWNS

London	Edinburgh	372 miles
London	Oxford	94 miles
Brighton	Manchester	245 miles
Bristol	York	214 miles
Cardiff	Glasgow	371 miles
Aberdeen	Exeter	555 miles

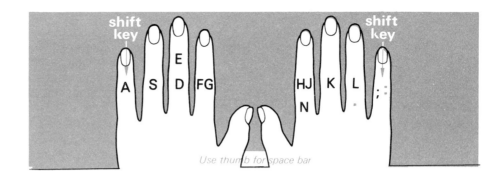

Use thumb for space bar

Revise keys learned

1 dde dee ded ffg fgg fgf jjn jnn jnj egn;

2 she has a faded jade fan and glass eggs;

3 a lass and lad held hands; dads kneeled;

Using the shift keys

Note the two large shift keys on the bottom row of the keyboard. These are for typing capital letters. When typing a left-hand capital letter, use the right-hand shift key, and vice versa.

When typing a *left-hand* capital letter:

1 Remove *right* hand from home keys and hold down *right* shift key with the little finger and the force of the hand behind it.   *Depress*

2 Type the required letter with the *left* hand.   *Strike*

3 Return the *right* hand to the home keys.   *Release*

Make sure you do not release the shift key until you have struck the letter—or the capital letter will not line up correctly. When you type right-hand capitals in line 12, follow the same procedure but use opposite hands.

Left-hand capitals
(use right shift key)

4 fF; Fan; Fell; Fake; dD; Dan; Dell; Dad;   *Sitting correctly?*

5 sS; Sand; Sell; Sad; aA; Ale; Ash; Anne;

6 gG; Gall; Gene; Gale; eE; End; Elk; Eel;

7 Sell; Dan; Ale; Fan; Dean; Elf; A; Gale;

8 All seed; Dead end; Sea shell; Gas leak;

use L finger
Strike full stop lightly

9 ll. ll. ll. l.. l.. l.. l.1 l.1 l.1 l..1

10 Sell a hen. Deal a hand. End all gags.   Tap two spaces after a full stop

11 Add sea shells. Gag lags. Fake a lead.

Right-hand capitals
(use left shift key)

12 jJa Jag; Jen; Jake; kKa Ken; Kale; Keen;

13 lLa Lake; Len; Lad; hHa Hag; Heel; Hand;   ; and shift key = : (colon)

14 nNa Nag; Neal; Nan; ;:a Leg: Jane: Held:

15 Handle shells. Lend nags. Keg all ale.

16 Jag lads. Nan sells jade. Lend a hand.

Prepare the typewriter

1 **'Clear' the typewriter** Move the margin stops out of the way, to the extreme right and left positions; and clear any existing tab stops.

2 **Insert your paper** Ensure that the left-hand edge is at 0 on the paper scales. Then turn up, from the top of the paper, the number of lines of space that you worked out in 4c on page 113.

3 **Move printing point** to the centre of the paper.

4 **Setting the left-hand margin position** (where each item in the first column will begin).
You will now need to apply horizontal centring but with this difference: it has to be adapted from the centring of an ordinary line of type to the centring across the page of a line of columns. The secret is to realize that the columns, together with the blank space between them, have to be regarded in the same way as unbroken lines of type across the page.

a   Decide which is the widest item in each of the columns—and put a mark against it.
b   From your position at the centre of the paper, backspace once for every two characters in each of these longest items and in the spaces to be left between

columns. Start with the first column and proceed, column by column, across the page. Say the characters to yourself in pairs as you do this. If an odd character is left after one column, carry it over to the next column or space. (When there is an odd character at the end, ignore it.)
c   Set your left-hand margin stop at the position arrived at—the starting point of the first column.

5 **Setting tabular stops for starting points of other columns**

a   Beginning at the left-hand margin, tap the space bar once for each character in the widest item of the first column. Then tap once for each space between the first and second columns.
b   Set your first tab stop at this point—the point you will begin typing each item in the second column.
c   From this first tab-stop position, tap the space bar once for each character in the widest item in the second column. Then tap once for each space between the second and third columns.
d   Set your second tab stop at this point—the point you will begin typing each item in the third column.
e   Continue in the same way for the remaining columns in the tabulation.

Type the tabulation

Your typewriter is now set for speedy and accurate placing of columns. *Type each complete line in turn.* Do *not* type columns vertically, one by one.

1   Type main headings, starting at left-hand margin. Leave vertical spacing decided on when making calculations.

2   Beginning at the left-hand margin position, type the first item in the first column, and then, using the tabulator, type the rest of the line.

3   Repeat the procedure until all horizontal lines in the table have been typed.

Paper scales				
	A4 portrait	A5 landscape	A5 portrait	A6 landscape
Spaces across the page				
Elite (12 to 1 in)	100	100	70	70
(centre point of paper)	50	50	35	35
Pica (10 to 1 in)	82	82	58	58
(centre point of paper)	41	41	29	29
Lines down the page (elite and pica both 6 lines to 2.5 cm or 1 in)	70	35	50	25

(**Note:**   With the above figures, you can allocate on your paper any space of specified size, eg for the later addition of an illustration. You would refer to the paper bail scale for horizontal measurement and use line-spacing for vertical measurement. You will need to do this in Unit 60.)

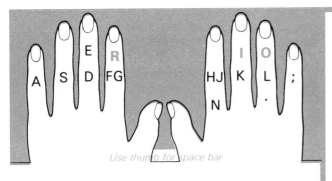

Use thumb for space bar

Finger and hand exercises Prepare the fingers for typing by practising the following exercises:

1 Alternately wring the hands tightly and shake the loosened fingers from the wrists.

2 Spread the fingers of both hands as wide as possible. Then close them and, starting with the little fingers, spread them one after another as widely as possible. Finally, relax the fingers and lightly form a fist.

Also practise the exercises when the finger muscles are tired after typing.

Revise keys learned

```
 1   11. 11. 11. 1.. 1.. 1.. 1.1 1.1 1.1 1..1
 2   Jan feeds hens; and sells eggs and kale.
 3   Deanna has a keen sense: and lean hands.
```
One space after ; and :

use K finger

```
 4   kki kki kki kii kii kii kik kik kik kiik
 5   hike hikes hiked like likes liked did in
 6   kill sill fill gill jail sail hail fails

 7   Diana said killing inside jail is a sin.
 8   Ian fails in singing: Gillian in hiking.
```
Little fingers for shift keys

R

use F finger

```
 9   ffr ffr ffr frr frr frr frf frf frf frrf
10   frail fried free rake rail reel reek ran
11   ark dark larks jerk dear near jeer sneer

12   Frieda likes fine rings and red dresses.
13   Fresh fish is dear and hares are dearer.
```
Eyes on copy

O

use L finger

```
14   llo llo llo loo loo loo lol lol lol lool
15   loll loss logs dog jog fog hogs rod hods
16   load loans loaf food hood good folk dose

17   Loss of good looks is no joke for Rosie.
18   Fresh roes on a long loaf are good food.
```
Use a sharp, even touch

Feet firmly on floor?

Use keys learned

```
19   Jones feared for his life on dark roads.
20   Idleness is foolish; learn a good skill.
21   Dense fog fell on hills and dales alike.
```

(Additional material on page 15)

What is tabulation?

In tabulation work you are required to type material (which may include figures) in the form of a 'table', in columns across the page. For pleasing and effective display, the tabulation should be centred horizontally and vertically on the paper. The blank space between columns should be equal, and the line spacing in the main part of the tabulation should be consistent.

The techniques used in tabulation are essentially those which you have already practised in horizontal and vertical centring for display. A ready knowledge of the figures relating to paper scales is vital for successful tabulation work. Therefore they are given again, for convenient reference, at the end of this Technique Section.

To type this tabulation:

	PRECIOUS/SEMI-PRECIOUS STONES			13th line from top of A5 landscape
	②			
	Amethyst	(3) Garnet	(3) Opal	
Leave 3 spaces between columns	①			
	Aquamarine	Jade	Pearl	
	①			
	Diamond	Jasper	Ruby	
	①			The table will occupy 10 lines in all
	Emerald	Onyx	Sapphire	

Measure the tabulation

1 **Decide size of paper** Consider the general shape of the tabulation. A short but wide one would be best suited to A5 landscape, and a narrow one to A5 portrait. Use your judgement whether the width and length together require the use of A4 paper. Often, of course, you will have to use the size of paper instructed.

2 **Decide blank space between columns** In any one piece of tabulation, the space between columns should always be the same. The ideal is three, four, or five character spaces. With any wider gap it becomes difficult to relate at a glance the information across the columns; with less than three spaces, the work tends to look cramped, and is less readable. In the early stages of your typing of tabulations, a good working rule will be to leave three character spaces.

3 **Decide vertical space between lines** The main body of the tabulation is usually typed in single or double spacing. Judge the material in relation to your size of paper, and make a note of the spacing you decide on.

4 **Make vertical calculations**

a Count the number of lines that the whole tabulation will occupy.
b Subtract this figure from the total number of lines down the paper.
c Divide the answer by two—for equal space above and below the tabulation.

This is a brief restatement of vertical centring.

Leader dots

In some tabulations the lines in the first column vary considerably in length. In order to 'square' them up, leader dots (unspaced full stops) are used. This both improves the appearance of the work and helps to lead the eye across the page to the related matter in the other columns (see page 116).

a There is always one character space before leader dots begin.
b Leader dots must line up vertically with the longest line in the column.
c When a very long line is divided (using single spacing) leader dots are typed only on the last line.

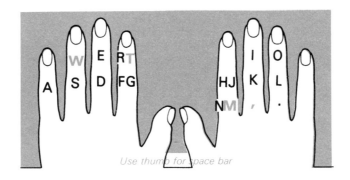

Use thumb for space bar

Revise keys learned

1 kki kii kik ffr frr frf llo loo lol iro;

2 Old fools jeer: daring soldiers ride on.

3 Her girls like red roses and gold rings.

M

use J finger

4 jjm jjm jjm jmm jmm jmm jmj jmj jmj jmmj   'Think' the finger you use

5 jam jams jammed jamming elm gem hem hems

6 rim him dim dims dimming home some domes

7 Miriam made me more lime and lemon jams.

8 Mr Jim Hammond mends frames for farmers.   Capitals lined up?

W

use S finger

9 ssw ssw ssw sww sww sww sws sws sws swws

10 swam was wall saw laws we well were when

11 swim swims swimming wise won woods wool;

12 Win will wed Owen Wise when work allows.

13 While walking in Wormwood we saw an owl.

T

use F finger

14 fft fft fft ftt ftt ftt ftf ftf ftf fttf   Return carriage sharply without looking up

15 fat fate mat mate set jet let met it fit

16 kit kite dot lot not note foot loot seat

17 Thomas told a tall tale to Tessa Tinker.

18 Lottie took a rest while Katie made tea.

,

use K finger

19 kk, kk, kk, k,, k,, k,, k,k k,k k,k k,,k   Strike comma lightly

Use keys learned

20 Sam, Kim and John were all good friends.   One space after comma

21 Make me an omelette, with milk to drink.

22 Her father is Danish, her mother German.

(Additional material on page 15)

In their advertisement, Brent & Rogers (Carriers) Ltd of 24/28 High Street claimed 'lowest rates in the City'. Yet they charged £50.50 to remove my few bits of furniture only 2 miles! What do you think of that?

1 *Technique Section 22 (page 111)*

a On a sheet of A4 paper, type the examples showing Roman numerals in *a*, *b* and *c*.
b On the same sheet of paper, type the passage about hanging paragraphs.

2 Type the following passage, using double spacing and indented paragraphs. (3 ringed errors to correct.)

Jeremy Jones has ~~only~~ just published ᵖart III (volumes vi to ix)

of his HISTORY OF ENGLAND. Part III covers the Tudor period from

Elizabeth I to Henry VII.

In Chapter XII there is a brilliant assessment of Henry VIII, while

Chapter XVI contains a ~~shrewd~~ clever character study of Queen Elisabeth I. The

Introduction to Part III of HISTORY OF ENGLAND is noteworthy. In the

ⁱIntroductory pages, viii to xiii, the author traces the social history

of the time. The religious struggles, fully deals with in the body of

the work, are also summarised with great clarity in pages xiv to xxv of

the Introduction.

3 Type the following examination hints as hanging paragraphs. Set the left-hand margin for the body of the paragraphs.

EXAMINATION HINTS
Go into the examination room with a sense of confidence.
You will achieve this if you know what to expect & if you
know that you can complete the test in the time allowed.
Therefore ~~carefully~~ work through ʌseveral past papers of (under examn conditions,)
the examn you are taking before you sit it.
(line of space) (preliminary typing) A day or two in advance, assemble in a folder all the
items you should take with you into the examn (pencil,
ballpoint pen, blank paper for rʌpractice, eraser, etc).
Arrive at the examn room in good time so you can prepare
yr typewriter, chair, etc ~~before the examn~~. This will
(help) ~~enable~~ you to start the examn in a relaxed mood :
and increase your chance of success.

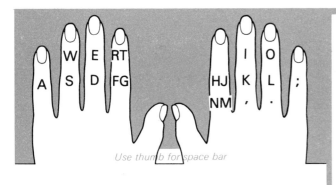

Use thumb for space bar

Instructions

Check fingering with the diagram before starting to type.

Copy each sentence and paragraph at least twice, as usual. Aim to increase speed, fluency and accuracy with each repetition.

The other instructions and technique points on pages 8 and 9 still apply. So quickly check them again.

Revise keys learned

1 jjm jmm jmj ssw sww sws fft ftt ftf mwt,

2 Jan wore a light dress: Kim a straw hat.

3 Mo told Wilma that the new jam was made.

One-line sentences

4 Get me a tin of milk from the new store.   Use a sharp even touch

5 We will see the old film this afternoon.

6 If it rains, meet Harold in the shelter.   One space after comma

7 Edith likes to make flower arrangements.

Longer sentences

8 Ann wrote her friend, Jim, a long letter   'Think' the
   telling him all she had seen in Ireland.   finger you use

9 It is good to see foreign goods on offer
   here, while we sell lots in other lands.

10 Martha likes sewing and has made herself
    skirts and hats as well as other things.

11 Whilst all golfers like the game in warm
    weather, some are as keen in winter too.

12 Her friends, Kate and Joan, are going to
    join the Fen Tennis Team that was formed
    in Newtown at the wish of John S Harman.

Short paragraphs

13 If we go home tired from work, the first   Two spaces
    thing we do is rest. After that we take   after full stop
    a stroll and then it is time for dinner.

14 We had to wait indoors all the afternoon
    as it rained so hard and the wind was so   Eyes on copy
    wild. Later on, we went to the theatre.

15 When all is said and done, this regiment
    was one of the finest. While others won
    more medals, none won more lasting fame.

Roman numerals

The Romans used a quite different system from the Arabic numbers we use today. All Roman numerals are derived from the seven letters I (one), V (five), X (ten), L (fifty), C (one hundred), D (five hundred) and M (one thousand).

Where the same numerals are repeated, they are added together: thus III is 3 and CC is 200. Where a smaller numeral follows a larger one, it is also added: thus VI is 6 and MD is 1500. Where a smaller number precedes a larger one, it is subtracted: thus IV is 4 and CM is 900.

When typed under each other, Roman numerals should be lined up, either to the right or to the left. This is illustrated below.

Examples of Roman numerals

(shown as *small Roman*)   (shown as *large Roman*)

1	i	6	vi		11	xi	16	xvi		30	XXX
2	ii	7	vii		12	xii	17	xvii		40	XL
3	iii	8	viii		13	xiii	18	xviii		339	CCCXXXIX
4	iv	9	ix		14	xiv	19	xix		988	CMLXXXVIII
5	v	10	x		15	xv	20	xx		1962	MCMLXII

(*lined up to the left*)   (*lined up to the right*)

Current uses of Roman numerals   Although Roman numerals are now seldom used, there are some uses which, by custom, continue in the language.

a   Roman numerals, large and small, may be used to number sections, sub-sections, etc, in various kinds of documents.

In support of his argument, Counsel for the Defence quoted The Social Security Pensions Act 1975, Section III, Sub-section iv.

b   Large Roman numerals are used to designate monarchs.

After the Union of the Crowns of England and Scotland in 1603, King James VI of Scotland became King James I of England.

c   Roman numerals are sometimes used to number school classes or forms, examination stages, sports teams, etc.

The Headmaster of Redcastle School announced at the Parents' Association meeting that German classes would, in future, be available to Forms V and VI, for examination at Stage I and Stage II.

Hanging paragraphs

With hanging paragraphs, the first line 'overhangs' the second and following lines by 2 spaces to the left.

Since most of the lines will be typed starting 2 spaces to the right of the first line, the left-hand margin should be set at this position to save time. The margin release key and the backspacer should be used together for typing the first line of each new hanging paragraph.

Hanging paragraphs are used mainly for sub-paragraphs, frequently with numbering. This passage is in the form of hanging paragraphs.

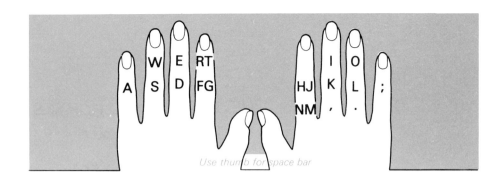

Use thumb for space bar

Unit 2
(Home keys and H)

1 a lad had a sad fall; all dads had fads;
2 a lass had a sash; dad had alaska salad;
3 all ash falls; slash a sash; add jaffas;   Brisk, even strokes
4 a sad lass shall dash as all halls fall;
5 all lads had jaffas; a lass has a salad;

Unit 3
(New keys E G N)

1 lean and aged hags fell dead as he fled;
2 lend a keen hand and sell sage and kale;
3 flash lads handle jade; she leases land;   Eyes on copy
4 gales lashed lakes and seas as she sang;
5 she sells sea shells; he needs a saddle;

Unit 5
(New keys I R O)

1 I relish good fresh air and dislike fog.
2 The herald angels sang songs for a King.
3 Ringo likes sailing; also riding horses.
4 All roadside hedges are fresh and green.
5 Sailor Sid has Rosie as his girl friend.

Unit 6
*(New keys M W T
Comma)*

1 Wait, James. No, I will not. Go, then.   One space after ,
2 Lassie, to heel. Here, sit. Down, dog.   Two spaces after .

3 I was the first to translate the letter.
4 He met, and liked, the new team fellows.
5 Slimming is good for health, it is said.
6 She delights in the shade of dark woods.
7 I like to swim when the weather is warm.

Additional practice material   Units 2 3 5 6   **15**

THE COACH AND HORSES INN
Lanchester
Dinner Menu

Tomato Soup
Fresh Grapefruit
Prawn Cocktail

* * *

Roast Beef and Yorkshire Pudding
Roast Chicken with Bread Sauce
Aylesbury Duckling with Orange Sauce

(AYLESBURY)

* * *

Roast and Boiled Potatoes
Cauliflower
Garden Peas
Baby Carrots

* * *

Fresh Fruit Salad
Cherry Tart
Lemon Cheesecake
Chocolate Gateau
with
Cream

* * *

Coffee or Tea

(on A4 with each line centred)

14 Type the same menu again, this time on A5 (portrait) paper. Use the blocked style of layout and extend the asterisks (or hyphens) as far as the longest item in the course above.

You must improve speed and accuracy together. There is no value in fast typewriting that is full of errors; nor in very slow typewriting, however accurate.

In each unit from now on, you will have speed/accuracy (S/A) practice. Its benefit will show in all your typewriting.

1 **Standard words** In speed/accuracy practice, words are counted as 'standard words'. A standard word consists of five strokes: each letter, character (punctuation mark or other sign) and space counts as one stroke. Therefore, in a typing line of 50 strokes there are 10 standard words; in a typing line of 60 strokes, 12 standard words, and so on.

The scale beneath each S/A passage divides the line into standard words to help you work out your speed.

2 **Use known material** It is easier to improve speed and accuracy on known material. Therefore, before starting your speed/accuracy timings, type the S/A passage at least once.

3 **Four-step practice** to increase speed and improve accuracy. The four steps are illustrated in part 4 below. Return the carriage twice after each step—to keep them clearly separated.

Step 1: *Control*

a Type the S/A passage for precisely one minute, repeating the passage until the timing is up. Type at your highest controlled speed, ie the highest speed at which you can maintain reasonable accuracy.

b Check your work by drawing a ring round each error. If a word contains more than one error, ring only the first one—and disregard the others. This is the examination method of correcting.

c Count the number of standard words typed.

d Record in the margin the number of ringed errors. Add, in brackets, the number of standard words typed. Thus, if you made two errors in 15 standard words, you would record **2 (15).** In front of these figures, add the letter C for Control— **C 2(15)**

Step 2: *Increase speed* (ignore errors)

a Type the same passage for precisely one minute, now aiming for increased speed even though you may make more errors.

b Count the number of standard words typed.

c Record this with an S (for Speed) in the margin, eg **S22.**

Step 3: *Force speed* (ignore errors)

a Type the same passage again for exactly one minute, this time in a determined drive to push your speed above that reached in step 2, even though the number of errors may rise again. But do not degenerate into typing so haphazardly that you produce senseless matter, full of errors.

b Count the number of standard words you have typed.

c Record this with an S in the margin, eg **S26**

Step 4: *Control*

a Type the passage yet again for precisely one minute. In this step, drop back to your highest controlled speed, ie the highest speed at which you can maintain reasonable accuracy.

b Check your work and ring any errors as you did in step 1.

c Count the number of standard words typed.

d Record in the margin the number of ringed errors. Add, in brackets, the number of standard words typed. In front of these figures, add the letter C for Control.

With this dual-purpose practice you should find that your final timing is not only faster but also more accurate than the first one. Your confidence will grow, and your combined speed/accuracy will improve in all your work.

In a class, the teacher will control S/A training. On your own, you can time yourself with a stop-watch, but it is better to get someone else to time you.

4 **Checking your work** Your first S/A practice may look like this:

(Step 1)
When the sun sh(u)nes, he likes to work in the open.   C2 (15)
When the s(j)n shines, he li

(Step 2)
When the sjn shines, he liked to work in the open.   S22
When the sun shines, he likes to wirk in the open.
Whej the s

(Step 3)
When the sun shines he liked to work in the open.   S26
When the suj shines, he likes to work in the open.
When the sun shines, he likes

(Step 4)
When the sun shines, he likes to work in the open.   C1(19)
When the sun shines, h(d) likes to work in the op

Target time: 4 minutes

Memo with cc
Please mark it URGENT

From Managing Director
To Works Manager, Ashton Yard

In the course of the next week I shd like to make a tour of the offices & the timber-yard to see & talk to as many as possible of our employees at their work.

(TIMBER)

while

Wd you please draw up a suitable programme & hold yrself free to accompany me.

cc and DL envelope
– for despatch today

Target time: 12 minutes

Mr A Walsh
The Limes, Langton Avenue, CHELTENHAM CH2 4BD

Dr ~~Mr Walsh~~ Sir

SALE OF THE LIMES, LANGTON AVE

last Wednesday

Following our visit to you, we enclose a copy of the particulars drawn up about yr house. You will see that we have stressed particularly the advantages of its situation. There is no doubt that many buyers will be interested in yr ~~house~~. However, to ensure

property

that we get the best offer we can quickly, we shall advertise in both the local newspapers this weekend.

number

// We expect a no of prospective buyers will wish to view the house on Saturday & Sunday & we will telephone you to make the necessary arrangements. However if you have to go away – as you said was possible – it wd be most helpful if you cd arrange to leave a key with a neighbour: all viewers wd, of course, be escorted.

We look forward to hearing from you.

Yours ffly

ZENITH ESTATE AGENCY

Date	S/A No	Length of Timing	First Control Timing	Highest Speed Timing	Final Control Timing
26 May	1	1 min	C 2 (15)	S 26	C 1 (19)
28 May	2	1 min	C 2 (18)	S 28	C 1 (22)
20 July	27	2 mins	C 3 (30)	S 40	C 2 (32)

5 **Record your performance** You will find it useful and stimulating to record the results of your S/A training.

6 **Syllabic intensity** You will see that against each S/A passage an SI count is given. Syllabic intensity is the average number of syllables in the actual words in the passage. For instance, in the sentence 'When the sun shines, he likes to work in the open' there are 11 actual words and the total number of syllables is 12. Therefore the syllabic intensity (SI) is 1.09 (12 syllables, 11 actual words; $12 \div 11 = 1.09$).

As a general rule, the higher the SI, the more difficult is the content of the passage: it has been estimated that the average syllabic count is about 1.40.

To make this clearer, consider the following difficult sentence which has the very high SI of 3.00 (27 syllables, 9 actual words). 'Inexperienced candidates possessing minimum qualifications seldom secure good positions.'

There has to be a recognized standard of difficulty for speed/accuracy work—so that the results achieved on different passages can be meaningfully compared with one another. Counting 'standard' words instead of actual words is one method used; another is the use of a common measure of syllabic intensity.

7 **Maintain your good typewriting habits** Never sacrifice good typewriting habits (the way you sit and do things) for the sake of obtaining greater speed and accuracy. Good techniques are the sure foundation on which to build sound typewriting skill—that is why they are so continually stressed in this book.

8 **Set your own goals** In your S/A training you should aim to improve, gradually but steadily, the speed and quality of your typing. If you are in a class, do not be distracted if others seem to be doing much better than you. Some people achieve high speeds more quickly than others in straightforward copying work of this kind. Just set your own goals and work to your best ability to improve on your own best performance.

You will not always find that your performance improves. Ups and downs are a well-known feature of day-by-day typing practice. So do not be disappointed if this sometimes happens. Look at your week-by-week results for a truer picture.

The flags waved gaily in the June breeze as the King and Queen's coach appeared exactly on time.

1 *Technique Section 21 (page 104)*

On A4 paper type the list of business forms (*a* to *i*) but *do not* type the letters. Use margins of 2.5 cm (or 1 in) and single spacing, double between items. Use initial capitals and underscoring for the names of the forms at the left-hand margin.

In each case leave three spaces between the name of a form and its following description. These are *paragraph headings*—which you will learn more about on page 118. Type a blocked heading *DOCUMENTS USED IN BUSINESS TRANSACTIONS*.

2 Type the following statement of account:

STATEMENT

International Book Company Limited
86-90 Kings Parade
CHESTER CH3 2BQ

To: Westons Bookshop
16 Main Road
LEICESTER
LR6 4PA

Date: 30 April 19--

Fo 96

Terms: Net 30 days

Date	Ref		Debit	Credit	Balance
19--			£	£	£
31 March		Balance			987.50
6 April	2396	Goods	260.50		1,248.00
10 April	2486	Goods	288.50		1,536.50
12 April		Cheque		987.50	549.00
18 April	C 961	Returns		23.60	525.40
24 April	2601	Goods	350.25		875.65

3 Type another Statement of Account for the International Book Company Limited, using the same date. It is to their customers Smart Bros, 46 High Street, OXFORD OX3 2BQ. Fo 102.

Date	Ref		Debit	Credit	Balance
31 March		Balance			205.87
4 April	2106	Goods	186.20		392.07
10 April	2487	Goods	320.40		712.47
18 April	2763	Goods	75.80		788.27
18 April	C 962	Returns		17.70	770.57
20 April		Cheque		205.87	564.70
25 April	2968	Goods	54.60		619.30

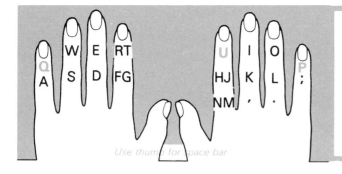

Use thumb for space bar

Instructions

Left margin: elite 25, pica 15   (Units 8, 9 and 10)

In this unit you will start speed/accuracy training (line 21). This is explained in Technique Section 2 (page 16).

Revise keys learned	1	Alison, Daniel, Esther, Ferdinand, George, Harold,
	2	Irene, Jennifer, Kenneth, Leonard, Martha, Norman,
	3	Oswald, Rosalind, Samantha, Theodore and Winifred.

P

use semi colon finger

4 ;;p ;;p ;;p ;pp ;pp ;pp ;p; ;p; ;p; ;;p ;pp ;p; pp
5 lap; sap; pads; spade; spades; weep; sweep; sweeps
6 sip; lip; pin; pride; kipper; fop; lop; sop; rope;

7 Pam slipped pen, paper and an apple into the pram.
8 In the sprint, he pipped his opponent at the post.

U

use J finger

9 jju jju jju juu juu juu juj juj juj jju juu juj uu
10 jug jut just jute dull hull full pull gull sun nun
11 sung hung dust must rust pun fun hum rum sum under

12 For supper Lulu pulled jugfuls of pure pump water.
13 Our Aunt Una just put lumps of turnip in our soup.

Q

use A finger

14 aaq aaq aaq aqq aqq aqq aqa aqa aqa aaq aqq aqa qq
15 quakes quads squares squeals quell requests queens
16 quit quire require quote quota liquor equal equate

17 Quentin lent me a quaint square hat, with sequins.
18 The frequent request of the Quakers was for quiet.

Use keys learned

19 In his wig and gown, the judge stood up and spoke.
20 More than a quarter of the students took the test.

SI 1.09

S/A 1 (1 minute) ●   21 When the sun shines, he likes to work in the open.

| | 1| | 2| | 3| | 4| | 5| | 6| | 7| | 8| | 9| | 1 0| |

(Additional material on page 21)

As the sad nun fed the pony, Vera started her car and gave a look of great joy.

1 *Technique Section 21 (page 104)*

Pay special attention to the information about credit notes.

2 Type the following credit note:

CREDIT NOTE

International Book Company Limited
86-90 Kings Parade
CHESTER CH3 2BQ

No 961

To: Westons Bookshop
16 Main Road
LEICESTER
LR6 4PA

Date: 18 April 19--

Reason for Credit	Quantity and Description	Unit cost	Amount
		£	£
Goods returned (pages missing)	3 Secretarial Practice - A Winton (Fanfare)	4.20	12.60
Goods damaged - 50% reduction	4 James Burton - A Biography (Sanderson)	5.50	11.00
	Total Amount Credited		£23.60
E & OE			

3 Type two more credit notes for the International Book Company Limited, using the same date.

a Smart Bros, 46 High Street, OXFORD, OX3 3BQ. Credit Note No C 962. Goods returned damaged, 3 copies The Wines of Europe—T Prince (Fanfare) @ £4.50 amounting to £13.50. Goods returned damaged, 1 copy Silent Waters—A Browning (Sanderson) @ £4.20. Total amount credited £17.70.

b Aztec Book Co Ltd, 18 Meadow Lane, DERBY DE4 3XV Credit Note No C 963 Goods returned faulty, 2 copies Dressmaking for Style - G Grace (Everest) @ £6.00 amounting to £12.00. Goods damaged - 50% reduction, 4 copies Gardening for All - C Davis (Long) @ £7.00 amounting to £14.00. Total amount credited £26.00.

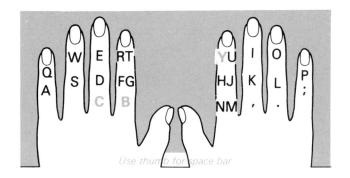

Use thumb for space bar

Revise keys learned

1   ;;p ;pp ;p; jju juu juj aaq aqq aqa ;p; juj aqa p;

2   This afternoon, Kim will go to a department store.

3   The order is: girls to remain indoors; lads to go.

B

use F finger

4   ffb ffb ffb fbb fbb fbb fbf fbf fbf ffb fbb fbf bb

5   fab jab dab ban ball web pebble bell fib fibs nibs

6   rib bid bib big fob sob lob mob boss dub rub bulbs

7   Babs and Billie liked to blow big, bright bubbles.

8   His big brother built a barn in timber and pebble.

Y

use J finger

9   jjy jjy jjy jyy jyy jyy jyj jyj jyj jjy jyy jyj yy

10   jay jays day days pays paying yawn yap yes yet yen

11   grey prey fry frying joys boys soya you your yours

12   Buy as many yards in red as they say you may need.

13   By day you may see my boy at play with young Gary.

C

use D finger

14   ddc ddc ddc dcc dcc dcc dcd dcd dcd ddc dcc dcd cc

15   decks pecks sack hack crack lice rice diced priced

16   cock mock sock lock suck luck ducked cycled crocks

17   Acrobatic clowns cycle in circles in circus rings.

18   Carrying coals to Newcastle causes constant chaos.

Use keys learned

19   It is just a saying: when in doubt, best left out.

20   Queen Karen came in splendour to the royal palace.

SI 1.00

S/A 2 (1 minute)

21   If you get a fly or a sty in your eye, do not cry.

| | 1| | 2| | 3| | 4| | 5| | 6| | 7| | 8| | 9| | 10|

(Additional material on page 21)

It is a question of judgment how long any person can keep up concentration without becoming over-fatigued, and can relax without growing lazy.

1 *Technique Section 21 (page 104)*

Refresh your memory on business forms. Specially note the information about VAT.

2 Type the following invoice that includes VAT. Use today's date.

No 2374

Invoice

Southern Furnishings (Wholesale)

80–82 Christchurch Road

BOURNEMOUTH BH6 3DT

VAT Registration No. 431 2871 63   Date:

Sold to: Jennings & Harlow
86 Castle Road
SOUTHAMPTON SO3 4PL

Your Order No. F 187   Terms: **Net one month**

Tax point	Type of supply	Description	Unit cost	Amount	VAT rate	VAT amount
(use date above)			£	£		£
	Sale	6 Armchairs No 632	85.00	510.00	10%	51.00
"	"	1 Sideboard No 248	300.00	300.00	"	30.00
"	"	4 Desks No 143	150.00	600.00	"	60.00
"	"	5 Bookcases No 325	112.00	560.00	"	56.00
		Total Goods		1,970.00		197.00
		Total VAT		197.00		
E & OE		Total Amount Due		£2,167.00		

3 Type another invoice from Southern Furnishings (Wholesale) to Jennings & Harlow, this time for 2 each of the same items, at the same prices, as on the above invoice. Quote Invoice No 2499 and Order No F198. Date this second invoice one month later. Fill in the amounts and totals yourself.

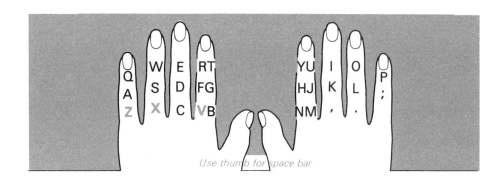

Use thumb for space bar

Revise keys learned

1 ffb fbb fbf jjy jyy jyj ddc dcc dcd fbf jyj dcd b;
2 James is the young club leader; Kenneth helps him.
3 Philip was bored by it all, and yawned frequently.

V

use F finger

4 ffv ffv ffv fvv fvv fvv fvf fvf fvf ffv fvv fvf vv
5 rave have gave ever lever dive jive live dove move
6 van vat vet vile villa vow valid very value vipers

7 Each villa has a very lovely view over the valley.
8 Sylvia and Vic have voices of average vocal value.

X

use S finger

9 ssx ssx ssx sxx sxx sxx sxs sxs sxs ssx sxx sxs xx
10 ax lax wax sex exit six mix fox box oxen crux flax
11 tax taxes taxi exist extra fixed mixed boxes boxer

12 The expert boxers were vexed at these extra taxes.
13 Rex used an axe to fix an extra post at each exit.

Z

use A finger

14 aaz aaz aaz azz azz azz aza aza aza aaz azz aza zz
15 laze lazy craze crazy size sizes dozen frozen buzz
16 zero zeal zip zinc zoo zoom fuzzy zebra azure haze

17 The crazy zealots had fuzzy hair and blazing eyes.
18 Zaza says that zeal brings endless zest to living.

Use keys learned

19 Bill should jump quickly over the gate of the zoo.
20 Invalids, avoid all undue exertion: and pressures.

SI 1.10

S/A 3 *(1 minute)*

21 The water from the pump was cool, pure, and clear.

| | 1| | 2| | 3| | 4| | 5| | 6| | 7| | 8| | 9| | 10|

(Additional material on page 21)

UNIT 10 V X Z (alphabet now complete) **20**

By just one reckless action in dropping a lighted match, an explosion and fire were caused which quickly razed the vast factory to the ground.

1 *Technique Section 21 (page 104)*

2 Type the following invoice:

INVOICE

No 2486

International Book Company Limited
86-90 Kings Parade
CHESTER CH3 2BQ

Sold to: Westons Bookshop
16 Main Road
LEICESTER
LR6 4PA

Date: 10 April 19--

Terms: Net 30 days

Quantity	Description	Unit cost	Amount
		£	£
20	James Burton - A Biography (Sanderson)	5.50	110.00
10	English Usage Today - B Lightfoot (Everest)	3.35	33.50
15	Secretarial Practice - A Winton (Fanfare)	4.20	63.00
20	Murder at the Inn - J Grant (Sanderson)	4.10	82.00
			————
E & OE			£288.50

3 Type two further invoices for the International Book Company Limited, using the same date. Use the invoice above as a guide for setting out.

a Sold to Smart Bros. 46 High Street, OXFORD OX3 3BQ. Invoice No 2487:
20 copies The Wines of Europe—T Prince (Fanfare) @ £4.50—£90.00;
15 ,,   Wales and Its Castles—D White (Long) @ £6.50—£97.50;
10 ,,   Good Grooming—S Shaw (Everest) @ £8.25—£82.50;
12 ,,   Silent Waters—A Browning (Sanderson) @ £4.20—£50.40.
These books total £320.40.

b Sold to Aztec Book Co Ltd, 18 Meadow Lane, DERBY DE4 3XV. Invoice No 2488:
50 copies Gardening for All—C Davis (Long) @ £7.00—£350.00;
20 ,,   Good English Cooking—M Allan (Everest) @ £4.35—£87.00;
15 ,,   Mystery of Moat Farm—P New (Sanderson) @ £3.35—£50.25;
10 ,,   Dressmaking for Style—G Grace (Everest) @ £6.00—£60.00.
These books total £547.25.

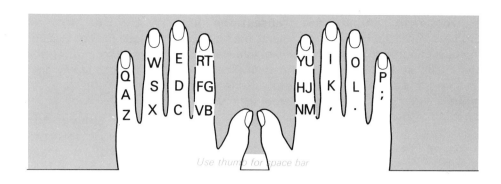

Use thumb for space bar

1 Question periods are useful at our staff meetings.

2 Paul thought it prudent to make his own enquiries.

3 Quarrelsome and proud students are most unpopular.

4 A proper square has equal sides with equal angles.

5 A glorious red sunset followed the afternoon rain.

6 Put the question to her. As she is unqualified in
languages, this post as an au pair in Europe would
seem useful and pleasant too. I would jump at it.

1 Caroline was simply lyrical about her new bicycle.

2 There are always bargains if you choose carefully.

3 Bob played for the local hockey and cricket clubs.

4 I quoted the saying that curiosity killed the cat.

5 Carole, come to the barbecue on Sunday if you can.

6 A square peg in a round hole is a figure of speech
to describe an ill fit: it could be a prim puss at
a discotheque, or the clumsy bull in a china shop.

1 Vera, please examine and repair this zip fastener.

2 Several villages were destroyed by the earthquake.

3 Everyone complains about the size of his tax bill.

4 Only an expert climber could survive such hazards.

5 The zebra was very excited, for no apparent cause.

6 Everyone knows that if you have grown lazy and big
in size, you need regular exercise. A little each
day is ideal; a daily dozen avoids undue exertion.

1 Documents in business transactions In a business transaction, various documents pass between the buyer and seller. As far as possible, forms are used and letters are kept to a standard pattern. This makes for speed and efficiency. Some typical business documents are described below in the order they would be used. All of them are not necessarily used in a single transaction.

If you are familiar with the commonest forms and can type them confidently and well, you should have no difficulty in dealing with any of the numerous variations to be found in different offices.

a Enquiry A purchaser asks a supplier for details of goods—qualities, colours, prices, delivery dates, etc. This may be by letter, but the requirements will be listed and set out very much as in a form.

b Quotation The supplier provides the information, either on a special quotation form or set out in a list within a letter.

c Order If the quotation is acceptable, an order will be placed for the goods desired. The purchasing firm might have its own printed order form, designed for its purposes generally. Or again, the order could just be set out in a letter.

d Advice note Upon despatch of the goods, some suppliers send the purchaser an advice note detailing the goods and stating the method of transport.

e Delivery note At the time of delivery, the buyer is given a delivery note describing the goods received; he signs a copy of it for return to the supplier, to indicate that the goods have actually been received.

f Invoice The supplier then sends the buyer an invoice. This records the transaction in detail, including quantity, description and price of the goods; it also states the amount due for them. Invoice forms are not always used. Some suppliers give the necessary information on ordinary letterheads.

g Debit note (or supplementary invoice) If an invoice proves to have been incorrect and the amount due was understated, this is pointed out by the supplier to the buyer in a debit note.

h Credit note If the goods listed in an invoice are returned as incorrect or faulty, the supplier sends the buyer a credit note for the cash difference. Credit notes are often printed in red to distinguish them from other documents.

i Statement of account In this, the supplier bills the buyer for payment. Statements of account are sent at regular intervals (often monthly). By a summary of the transactions, they show the amount due after adjustment for debit or credit notes and any payment(s) made since the last account was sent.

2 E & OE Many invoices and other business forms include the abbreviations E & OE (for *errors and omissions excepted*). This shows that the supplier reserves the right to rectify any errors and omissions that may come to light.

3 VAT (Value Added Tax) and invoices A trader who is registered for VAT and who supplies taxable goods to another taxable person must issue a tax invoice. This must include the following information, additional to the usual information supplied on an invoice.

a Seller's VAT registration number.
b Tax point, ie the date on which the goods were supplied.
c Type of supply—sale, hire, hire purchase, etc.
d Price of each item and the total for the goods (excluding VAT).
e Rate and amount of VAT chargeable for each item and the VAT total.
f Total amount due, ie the total for the goods plus the total for VAT.

As you will know, the VAT rate changes from time to time. For practice purposes, it is taken at 10%. Some goods, including books, are not subject to VAT.

4 Preparing forms for typewriting practice For practice in typing the various forms used in the next four units, you may need to prepare your own blank forms to type on. It will save time to type two or three forms at the same time, by making carbon copies. Use the illustration as a guide and draw your lines neatly on suitably sized paper, with a ruler and a black ball-point pen—after making guide lines or marks with a pencil. To do this successfully, you will find it helpful to clip the papers carefully together at top and bottom with slip-on paper clips—to prevent them from slipping.

5 Completing the forms Apply the skills you used when filling in forms in Units 43 to 47. When you come to type the information set out in columns, also apply the skill of typing figures in columns, which you practised in Unit 50.

Set your left-hand margin stop where the first column will begin and set tab stops for the starting position of the other columns. Use your judgement whether to use single, 1½ or double line spacing.

6 Positioning figures between vertical lines

Begin the first character in the column beneath the first letter of the heading.

Left margin: elite 20, pica 10 (Units 11 to 20)

Keep your typing of this unit for error analysis in Technique Section 3.

Revise alphabet

1 The crazy pavement was quickly fixed by a jolly old gardener.

Blocked paragraphs

2 In typing, there are different kinds of paragraph. They are called blocked, indented and hanging paragraphs.

3 Blocked paragraphs are now widely used in typing. They are the easiest and fastest to type.

4 With blocked paragraphs all lines, including the first, begin at the left margin. You are now typing blocked paragraphs: you also typed them at the end of the last consolidation unit.

Using the tabulator

Locate the following on your typewriter:

1 *Tab-set key* to set the position of tab stops.

2 *Tab-clear key* to clear a tab stop.

3 *Tab bar (or key)* to move the carriage direct to the tab stop positions, in turn.

To clear a tab stop you must move the carriage to the tab-stop position before pressing the tab-clear key. Some typewriters have a device for clearing all existing tab stops at once.

**Setting a tab stop
for indented paragraphs**

The first line of an indented paragraph begins five spaces to the right of all the other lines.

1 Clear all existing tab stops.

2 Tap the space bar five times from the left margin position.

3 Press the tab-set key to set a tab stop at this point.

At the beginning of each indented paragraph depress the tab bar (or key) so that the carriage moves direct to the correct position to start typing.

Indented paragraphs

5 As you will see, the first line in indented paragraphs begins to the right of the other lines. You should always use the tabulator to set and find the place where each first line begins. You are now typing an indented paragraph.

6 You are using single spacing in this unit and will see that there is no full line of space between the lines of type. You are using the carriage return twice between paragraphs: this gives a line of space between the lines of type.

7 You can now type both blocked and indented paragraphs. Later on you will learn how to type hanging paragraphs: these are used less often than blocked and indented ones.

SI 1.17

S/A 4 (1 minute)

8 When you type, you should keep your eyes mainly on the copy.

| 1 | 2 | 3 | 4 | 5 | 6 | 7 | 8 | 9 | 10 | 11 | 12 |

The judge thanked the witness for his lucid explanation of the events leading to the quarrel on the motor launch in Cadiz Bay.

1 *Technique Section 20 (page 102)*

On a sheet of A4 paper, type the examples given. Practise typing each one in turn, until you can copy them accurately and without hesitation. Do not be discouraged if you cannot do this immediately: typing of this kind requires great precision. With care and perseverance you will soon succeed.

2 On A5 portrait paper, type the following list of times in double spacing. Centre the list vertically. Begin typing the heading at the left-hand margin position, and leave two lines of space after it. Complete the second column yourself for 8.30 am and 6.00 pm.

Elite—left-hand margin 26; tab stop 37
Pica—left-hand margin 20; tab stop 31

<u>THE 24-HOUR CLOCK</u>

5.30 am	0530 hrs
8.30 am	
9.00 am	0900 hrs
Noon	1200 hrs
3.30 pm	1530 hrs
6.00 pm	
9.00 pm	2100 hrs

3 Type the following list on A5 landscape in double spacing. Leave two lines of space between the heading and the first item in the table. Centre the list vertically. Take care to line up the figures correctly in the third item.

Elite—left-hand margin 33; tab stop 60
Pica—left-hand margin 24; tab stop 51

PRINCIPAL HEIGHTS ABOVE SEA LEVEL
(in feet)

Africa: Kilimanjaro	19,340
Asia: Mount Everest	29,028
Australia: Kosciusko	7,316
Europe: Mont Blanc	15,782
New Zealand: Cook	12,349
North America: McKinley	20,320
South America: Aconcagua	22,834

Analyse your typing of Unit 11

To know your mistakes is a good part of the way to rectifying them.

Look at your typing of Unit 11. You are circling your errors so can quickly tell whether particular keys are causing you difficulty.

List your mistakes List all mistakes on a piece of paper. Add a cross each time the same error is repeated.

Your list may look like this (which would require special practice on E I Y and T).

Wrang Keys

E   X X X X
N   X
I   X X X X X
C   X
Y   X X X X
T   X X X X X
A   X
B
full stop   X
Comma   X X
S
K

Other faults

Faint letter   X X
Heavy letter
Two letters run together   X
Letters transposed
Raised capital letters   X X
Wrong spacing between words
Wrong spacing between lines
Wrong spacing after
     punctuation marks   X X
Uneven left-hand margin
Omission of letters   X
Omission of words
Omission of line   X

Rectify your errors

1 Some mistakes in typewriting may arise from faulty techniques, so check the important technique points on page 9.

2 *Practise problem letters and techniques* For any letter you need to improve, practise again the five lines given when that letter was first introduced. The five lines consist of:

a *one line of letter drill* to associate the new letter with its home key.

b *two lines of words* in which you will frequently use the new letter in a variety of combinations;

c *two sentences* that give further intensive practice of the new letter.

Additional material In Unit 1 (home keys) this pattern does not apply. However, on pages 24 and 25 there are paragraphs in which each letter on the home row (and E N) is intensively drilled. You will also find a carriage return drill, a space bar drill, a double-letter drill and a shift keys/comma drill, in case you need to improve any of these points.

Now work on each letter and technique that needs attention. Leave it and pass on to the next one only when you feel definite improvement.

You can then proceed with confidence to the typing of figures in Unit 12.

TECHNIQUE 3   Errors: analysis and action   **23**

1 **Figures in columns for calculation** Whenever numbers are typed in a column for the purpose of calculation, the units, tens, hundreds, etc, should be accurately lined up under one another, as they would appear in print. When typing columns, set a tab stop for the first figure of the longest line in the column and tap the space bar for any shorter lines.

2 **Lines above and below a total** Spacing and instructions are shown in the examples below. The interliner or variable line-spacer should be used to raise the paper slightly before typing the lower of the double lines.

Note that the lines above and below the total should stop short of the £ symbol in front of the total; and should not extend beyond the final figure on the right-hand side.

3 **Sums of money (pounds and pence) columns** If a column consists of amounts in pounds and pence, the decimal points must be typed in line. Examples follow:

	3a *Single spacing*	3b *1½ spacing*	3c *Double spacing*
	£	£	£
	100.05	246.85	268.43
	12.60	24.60	
	8.00		18.70
	24.86	2.76	
	.50	103.24	103.25
	£146.01	£377.45	£390.38

In the first amount of money in *a* above, .05 = 5p and in the last amount .50 = 50p. To avoid confusion in such cases, there should always be two digits following the decimal point. Note also in *a* that the £8 in the third amount is followed by two noughts—but the last item (50p) need not be preceded by a nought.

4 **£ symbol at head of column**

a Blocked style The £ symbol should be typed over the first digit (as in 3a above).
b Centred style The £ symbol may be placed over the decimal point (as in 3b above) or over the units column of pounds (as in 3c above). However, consistency on this point should be observed within a single piece of work.

5 **Sums of money (pounds only) in columns** It is not necessary to use the decimal point. In the blocked style of layout the £ symbol should be placed over the first digit of the longest line (as in *a* below). In fully centred display, it should be centred over the longest line in the column (as in *b* and *c* below). Examples in single, 1½ and double spacing follow:

a	£	*b*	£	*c*	£
	688,265		3 648 175		263 762
	168,120		235 684		
	8,135		5 120		14 928
	26,283		468		17
	146				
	£890,949		£3 889 447		£278 707

Letter A

Adam was a sad man after that car crash. Happily, no bad personal harm was caused, but the car was damaged past repair. Insurance value can be far less than it takes to replace a car that was a family favourite.

Letter S

Susan insists her silk dress is inches short. She always seems to see faults in clothes. Sometimes she says her jeans and sweaters must fit closer; just as often she wants them loose. Shoes and scarves seldom please Susan.

Letter D

Donald and David are good friends. In their hard days they had lived in bad conditions and learned to make do and mend. Skilled at handwork, they had made saddles and sundry wooden goods to order, and duly decided to adopt this as a trade.

Letter F

Before the first frosts, flocks of swifts form over our farm in the Norfolk Fens and fly off to the far fields of France. For our feathered friends who do not follow, it is often difficult to find, on frozen fenland, enough food for life.

Letter G

George is right in saying gifts are a sign of goodwill, the giver seeking no gratitude or advantage, nor wishing to encourage greed for belongings. A good thought in choosing a gift has greater meaning than a high charge paid.

Letter H

The chairman has high hopes that this mammoth housing exhibition will help both the home building and furnishing industries. Changing methods of house heating and new fashions in kitchen and bathroom equipment are on show.

Letter J

The subject was the hijacking of a Jersey to Majorca jet by Fuji Moji, said to be a Japanese adjutant on a war project. Judge Jeffrey rejected all but the plea of a juvenile mind. The jury adjourned for just an hour before the judgment.

Letter K

Kitty kept a kiosk by the lake, with cakes for the cricketers and coke for the kids. By a stroke of luck, Mick the Yank came by, in hacking jacket and check knickerbockers. Kate and Mike now keep chickens in Kentucky.

We have noted your change of address from 247 High Street to 398 Park Avenue. The 5 copies of our 60-page catalogue will be sent to you before 1 May. I must remind you that we have not yet received your cheque for £456.87 to cover our Invoice number G23901. This order for 4 tables and 24 chairs was despatched to you on 5 March on the understanding that payment would be made within 30 days.

Type the following memos on plain paper or on printed memo-heads. Take one carbon copy of each and use today's date.

a

MEMO
From Office Manager   Ref BW/LS
To   All Office Staff
PRIVATE TELEPHONE CALLS

Our telephone bills have risen sharply during the last yr. Some of this increase is obviously due to higher telephone charges.)
But it is evident that staff are more & more using the office telephone for personal calls — instead of making use of the coin-box telephones that are provided on most floors of the building. [When a member of staff uses an office telephone — & this is permissible only in an emergency — the call shd be made through the switchboard & paid for immediately. By using the ADC (Advise Duration and Charge) facility this can be done simply & accurately. [I am sure you will all co-operate in this matter.

b

MEMO to Miss J Packer from J Fountain   Ref JSF/bs
As you know, the management of the company hv hd nothing but praise for the high standard of typing throughout the Organization. But recently there hv been complaints of growing delays in answering letters to the Co. In most Depts the blame is being put squarely on the typing centre. [I know you have staffing problems but wd ask you to make a special effort to speed up all typing work. If necessary I will review the limits on overtime & consider some additions to yr staff. Give this some thought & come & see me next week so we can discuss yr views & proposals.

Letter L

Bill and Lally live in a little hamlet in the Willow Hills.
It is delightful to look on the yellow daffodils and lilies
along the blue lake. Across the sloping fields and vales,
tall steeples stand like lonely sentinels.

Letter E

The Weekend Review is excellent in content and extremely
well written and edited. Articles of general interest are
interspersed with stories of often real literary merit.
The serial is a feature and there are poems in each issue.

Letter N

Near the end of Nunnery Lane, behind the new recreation
centre, stands the ancient sandstone Convent of St Ninian.
No finer building can be seen in the entire region. The
nuns have done much for the needy in the town.

Shift keys

When my Aunt Mary married Uncle Jack they emigrated to
Gisborne on North Island, New Zealand. She soon became
homesick for her old home town, Herne Bay in Kent. They
have just sailed home on the liner, Queen Diana. On their
way back they visited India, Sri Lanka, Portugal and
France.

Carriage return
(really speed it up)

Thank
Thank you
Thank you for
Thank you for your
Thank you for your letter.

Space bar

a b c d e f g h i j k l m n o p q r s t u v w x y z a b c

**Shift keys
and comma**

Ann, Bob, Chris, Don, Edgar, Fred, George, Harry, Ivy, Jack,
King, Lord, Mark, Ness, Opal, Peel, Quinn, Ross, Shaw, Tass,
Uncle, Vogue, Whistler, Xanadu, Yoland, Zoe.

Double letters

We hope it will be possible for you to supply immediately
some additional jigsaw puzzles. They have been a big
success, real winners. We suggest you send, as soon as
possible, a further supply of wooden puzzles in the cottage,
poppy, and spinning wheel patterns. We are sorry to rush
you but are finding it difficult to meet demand for these
excellent goods.

Jane paid £26.56 for the shoes at Bourne & Sons and £18.75 for the handbag at Lambeth & Company. I saw the same items in Jolly & Long's window for only £25.50 and £16.43.

1 *Technique Section 19 (pages 98 and 99)*

a Type the memos given in parts 1 and 4 of the Technique Section on A5 printed memo-heads. Take one carbon copy of each.
b On plain A5 landscape paper, type the memo given in part 6 of the Technique Section. Begin typing on the seventh line from the top of the paper and use margins of 2.5 cm (or 1 in). Take one carbon copy.

2 Type the following memos on plain paper or using printed memo-heads. Take one carbon copy of each and use today's date.

a

MEMORANDUM
From Catering Manager   Ref BG/SP
To   All Members of Staff   Date
CLOSURE OF CANTEEN
W effect from next Mon the canteen will be closed for 3 wks.
As you will know, the canteen is in need of ~~extensive~~ modernization ✓
& redecoration. I had ~~very much~~ hoped that all necy work
wd have been carried out during last summer's 3-wk holiday break:
unfortunately, due to a last-minute misunderstanding, this
was not possible. [I apologise for any inconvenience you will be
caused but feel sure you will consider the forthcoming
improvements will more than compensate for it.

b

MEMORANDUM
From ~~Assistant~~ Accountant   Ref DW/as/12653
To Sales Manager   Date

W CHARLSTON & SONS LTD

This firm is now considerably above its credit limit &
no further orders can be accepted from them until a
(large) ~~considerable~~ part of their balance is cleared.

Since you have good personal contacts with the firm, I
shd be grateful if you wd send to them a tactful
letter.

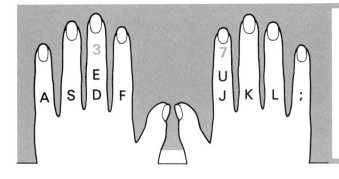

Instructions

Before you start typing a new figure, practise the movements from the home key and back.

Since complete accuracy in the typing of figures is vital, look at your typing line and keys if necessary, but *always use the correct finger.*

When checking your work, check any figures very carefully, one by one.

Revise alphabet

1   The quick, brown fox jumped right over the lazy, black dogs.

Start figures

3 *use D finger*

7 *use J finger*

2   de3ed de3d d3d de3ed de3d d3d: 3 duds 33 dots 3 dons 33 dogs

3   ju7uj ju7j j7j ju7uj ju7j j7j: 7 jugs 77 jars 7 jams 77 jigs

Practise 3 and 7

4   There were 737 seeds planted: but only 337 swedes took root.

5   Jack cut 73 cabbages, 7 marrows and 37 cucumbers in 3 weeks.

6   Sally moved from 3 Wood Road, London E7 to 73 Mill Lane, N3.

7   She baked 7 loaves, 3 jam rolls, 7 fruit cakes and 33 tarts.

8   On the farm there were 3 horses, 7 cows, 7 pigs and 33 hens.

Use 3 and 7 in blocked paragraphs

9   During the heatwave, we sold a record number of 73 pairs of
    sandals in 3 days. Our previous best was 37 pairs in 3 days.
    That was nearly 7 years ago.

10 Mary says that 7 people will be coming on the picnic on
    3 August. We shall meet at my house at 37 Park Close, and
    drive the 37 kilometres to Beechwood Forest in 3 cars.

11 On 7 June our local cricket team beat its greatest rivals
    by 373 runs to 337. Our captain went in to bat when 3
    wickets were down for 37, and saved the day with a fine
    innings of 73. After that our team scored steadily to the
    last man, who added a good 37.

SI 1.17

S/A 5 (1 minute)

12 Be sure that you use the right finger when you type figures.

| 1| | 2| | 3| | 4| | 5| | 6| | 7| | 8| | 9| | 1 0| | 1 1| | 1 2|

(*Additional material on page 30*)

UNIT 12   Figures 3 7   **26**

c Sometimes you may have to type particulars at the head of a memo over printed lines (dotted or unbroken). In that case, adjust your machine so that the alignment scale is a little above the line. The type will then be ideally positioned—just clearing the line.

4   *An A5 memo with printed memo-head and lines*

MEMORANDUM

From .....B G Walters..   *Ref* ...BGW/AS.......................................

To ....all Section Heads....................   *Date* ...(today's)....................................

CHRISTMAS BONUSES

It has been decided to give all staff the same generous Christmas bonus that they received last year - despite our adverse trading position at present.

Kindly inform all staff in your Section.

BW

5   **Memos without a printed memo-head**   Some organizations do not use printed forms for their memos. The typist then uses plain paper of suitable size and types in the necessary headings and information. The layout of memos varies considerably from firm to firm; however, this will present no problem once the basic form and purpose of memos is understood.

6   *An A5 memo without printed memo-head*

M E M O R A N D U M

To: Company Secretary   From: Managing Director

Date: (today's)   Ref: AL/bc

ANNUAL BOOKSELLERS' EXHIBITION AND DINNER

...   Further to our telephone conversation earlier today, I am attaching 2 tickets for tonight's Annual Booksellers' Exhibition and Dinner. Please note that the Exhibition will begin at 1730 hrs not 1830 hrs as stated on the tickets.

I have been unable to cancel my other engagement for this evening so should be most grateful if you and a guest would attend on my behalf.

AL

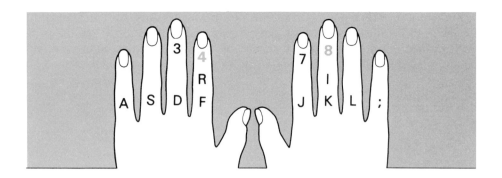

Type once paragraph 11 in Unit 12.

| 4 | use F finger | 1 | fr4rf fr4f f4f fr4rf fr4f f4f: 4 figs 44 feet 4 fees 44 fans |

| 8 | use K finger | 2 | ki8ik ki8k k8k ki8ik ki8k k8k: 8 kits 88 keys 8 kids 88 kegs |

Practise 4 and 8

3   Out of the 8 boys, 4 celebrated their 8th birthday on 4 May.

4   Bob has 48 flats to rent and 8 to sell: only 4 have garages.

Note the abbreviation for number

5   In order No 448 we asked for 4 pairs of gloves and 8 shirts.

6   The 8 crates contained 4 broken vases and 48 chipped plates.

7   Out of 848 buses, 48 broke down and 84 needed major repairs.

Use figures learned in indented paragraphs

8   For homework, read pages 38 to 47 of your Office Practice textbook. Also, carefully check the answers to your work on page 34. Study the diagram on page 87 for a test in the next lesson.

9   During the storm which swept Seacroft for 48 hours, 7 houses were damaged by falling trees and 78 by flooding. In all, 343 people were left homeless. It will take at least 7 or 8 weeks to repair all the damage.

10   Go to the general store at 48 High Street and buy 3 bars of soap, 4 packets of biscuits, 7 tins of soup and 8 candles. Then, from the greengrocer at No 73 in the same street, buy 8 bananas, 7 oranges and 4 lemons. Take back the 3 bad apples they gave you yesterday.

SI 1.07

S/A 6 (1 minute)   11   It is much better to walk to the shops than to drive by car.

| 1| 2| 3| 4| 5| 6| 7| 8| 9| 1 0| 1 1| 1 2|

(Additional material on page 30)

Memoranda, memorandums, or memos—as they are familiarly known—are written messages or communications between persons within an organization, usually within the same building or building complex.

Any of the standard paper sizes may be used for memos. Often the paper has a printed memo-head. Memos differ from letters in certain aspects of layout, which are explained below.

1   *An A5 memo with printed memo-head*

MEMORANDUM

From   Miss G Whitehouse   *Ref*   GW/AD/E12

To   Mr P Allen   *Date*   20 September 19--

COPY FOR NEW CATALOGUES

You said you would let me have the copy for your new catalogues by today at the latest. The stock of catalogues for your Section is nearly out - so the matter is urgent.

I have been unable to get you on the phone: they tell me you are on outside business most of this month. Do get in touch when you are next in the office and let me know the position.

GW

2   **General points**

a   There is no salutation or complimentary close, but it is clearly stated who is sending the memo, and to whom.
b   There is no inside address—obviously, since the sender and receiver work in the same organization.
c   As with letters, memos can have a subject heading—which is typed in the same way and position, above the body of the memo.

d   Like letters, memos can have a reference.
e   The memo is dated.
f   The style of English expression tends to be less formal in memos than is usual in business letters.
g   The sender has initialled the memo—which is common. Sometimes the signature is written in full.
h   A carbon copy is normally taken for the sender's file.

3   **Printed memo-heads**

a   The position of some information is governed by the printed heading.
b   Before typing these particulars in the space provided, first line up the base of the print with the align-

ment scale. Use the variable line-spacer for this purpose. Leave at least two character spaces between the print and the start of your typing. Preferably line up the items one under the other, as in the example.

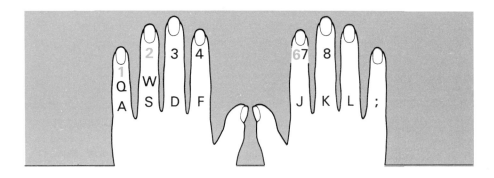

Revise figures learned   Type once paragraph 10 in Unit 13.

1 *use A finger*   1   aqlqa aqla ala aqlqa aqla ala: 1 aunt 11 arms 1 ally 11 ants

                        2   Bring out 111 forks, 11 spoons and 1 bowl from the cupboard.

2 *use S finger*   3   sw2ws sw2s s2s sw2ws sw2s s2s: 2 saws 22 sons 2 suns 22 sets
6 *use J finger*   4   jy6yj jy6j j6j jy6yj jy6j j6j: 6 jays 66 jobs 6 jets 66 jabs

Practise 1 2 6   5   John hit 26 and 21 runs: Alan 61 not out in just 66 minutes.

                        6   In the evening, 2 waiters and 6 waitresses served 61 guests.

                        7   After work buy 6 lemons, 2 melons, 12 oranges and 16 apples.

                        8   The 2 sums gave the same product: 2 times 66 and 6 times 22.

                        9   Buses No 11, 12, 16, 61 and 62 all pass close to your hotel.

Use figures learned in 10 Each of the following numbers can be evenly divided by 3 and
blocked paragraphs   6: 6, 12, 24, 48 and 72. In addition, the last 3 numbers
                            can be evenly divided by 8 and 12.

                        11 As well as my home and office telephone numbers, 738412 and
                            31462, numbers which I carry in my head are my Cheque Card,
                            876117, and my Automobile Association membership number,
                            81 16144 182.

                        12 On the first 3 days of our tour we covered 376, 481 and 467
                            miles. This took us into the mountains, where 126 and 87
                            miles were as far as we cared to travel in the next 2 days.
                            By a shorter return route we reached home in 2 daily stages
                            of 481 and 463 miles, making our total mileage 2,481 for the
                            tour.

                                                                            SI 1.05

S/A 7 (1 minute)   13 If you get a cheque card from your own bank you will be able
                            to cash cheques at most banks.

        | 1| 2| 3| 4| 5| 6| 7| 8| 9| 10| 11| 12|

                                            (Additional material on page 30)

10 Type the following passage on A4 paper in double or 1½ line-spacing, and with indented paragraphs. Centred heading ELECTRONIC TYPEWRITERS.

Target time: 18 minutes

Electronic typewriters have revolutionized typewriter operation. They perform automatically a range of functions ~~traditionally~~ *formerly* carried out ✓ by mechanical methods. For example, carrier return, underscoring, justified right-margin, *to text* and centring are all automatic.

And corrections are simple. A thin window display panel enables the typist to detect and correct errors in the text before *it is* committed to paper. Also, corrections for some way further back is easy: as the printhead back tracks to the point of error, the lift-off or cover-up correction tape is automatically brought into operation. After correction, the RELOC key returns the printing-point in a split second *to the last character typed* ~~for resumption of typing.~~ ✓

~~Some~~ Other useful features of electronic typewriters include: **backspacing versatility** – with express backtracking, or one character at a time, or in *very* small increments; **repeat typing** – for all keys; **ruling facility** – for both horizontal and vertical lines; **ribbon changes** quick and clean with the cassette system.

For quality *d*isplay layouts the facilities include automatic centring and justifying; emboldening; and variable typeface and pitch.

But perhaps the biggest step forward is the build*t*-in memory – which will automatically print out a*d*resses, signature block, short texts, etc, as well as reproduce page formats. *S*ome electronics have a memory of 8,000 characters (1,600 standard words). A double disc drive can be connected to some machines to double *their* memory to 16,000 characters. Th*u*s a list of names and addresses together with a standard letter could be entered into the memory and merged in print out for a mail-shot, etc. At this sophisticated stage, electronic typewriters begin to enter the realm of word processor facilities.

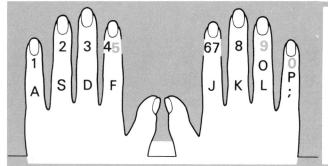

Hyphen and dash (used in nos 9 to 12)

The same key is used for the hyphen and dash. Find it on your typewriter and practise the movements from the home key and back before using it in no 9. Use the appropriate figure finger or the nearer little finger.

The *hyphen* is used in words made up from two or more other words. It has no space before or after it. The *dash* has a space before and after it.

Revise figures learned   Type once paragraph 12 in Unit 14.

5	*use F finger*	1	fr5rf fr5f f5f fr5rf fr5f f5f: 5 fins 55 fibs 5 fags 55 firs
9	*use L finger*	2	lo9ol lo9l l9l lo9ol lo9l l9l: 9 logs 99 lads 9 lots 99 laws
0	*use ; finger*	3	;p0p; ;p0; ;0; ;p0p; ;p0; ;0; 20 pages; 30 pills; 400 papers

Practise 5 9 0

4 Boys of 5 can run 50 metres in 55 seconds: men in 5 seconds.

5 If you add 9 and 90 you get 99: 9 plus 90 plus 900 make 999.

6 Order 90 locks and 95 keys for 90 doors in the 59 new flats.

7 Look for 5 or 55 for luck, but 50 or 950 will serve as well.

8 The 50 men built 9 houses, 9 garages and 5 shops in 90 days.

Hyphen

9 mother-in-law, Stratford-on-Avon, hitch-hiking, sons-in-law.

Use all figures (and hyphen/dash) in indented paragraphs

10 There are 365 days in a year or 366 in a leap-year. Each year has 12 months - 7 with 31 days and 4 with 30 days. February has 28 days or 29 in a leap-year.

11 We were booked to join Flight No XA804 - due to leave London at 1456 hrs. With 80 passengers disembarking and 35 joining, the plane was 75 minutes late leaving London and 90 minutes late in arriving at our destination.

12 With their 2-stroke engines roaring, the motor-cycles of the Red Devil Gang sweep nightly through the ill-lit streets of Greentown - a danger to their riders and to passers-by alike. The local Anti-Noise League consider this gang and their motor-cycle disturbance a top-priority cause for action - since all their warnings have gone unheeded.

SI 1.05

S/A 8 (1 minute)

13 When you use a shift key, be sure you do not release it till you have struck the right key.

| 1| 2| 3| 4| 5| 6| 7| 8| 9| 1 0| 1 1| 1 2|

(Additional material on page 30)

8 Type the following letter using today's date and taking one carbon copy. Type a DL envelope and clip the papers together, ready for signature.

Target time: 15 minutes

Borough Surveyor, Town Hall, LONGCHESTER LI5 2AS

Dr Sir

PAVEMENT IN HIGH STREET

or pass one another on it

I wish to draw yr attention to the poor condition of the pavement outside my bus. premises in the High St.

As you will be aware know, the pavement at this point is so narrow that it is scarcely possible for 2 people to walk abreast. At present this may be inevitable as the street itself is very narrow, but at least however the pavement shd be well maintained. As you must also know, however, it is often necy in this narrow street

(the)

for heavy lorries to mount this the pavement in order to pass vehicles coming from the opposite direction.

This has led to some of the paving stones becoming uneven or loose, so that the whole situation represents a severe serious danger to pedestrians. I very much hope you will ensure that is essential work is attended to without delay.

In addition, I hope you will expedite work on the proposed one-way traffic system round the centre of the town.

Yrs ffly

9 Type the following advertisement on A5 landscape paper. (2 ringed errors to correct.)

Target time: 10 minutes

THE COMPLETE ENGLISH DICTIONARY

Comprehensive but Consise

Conveniently Compact

Classified Contents

Centre each line

Supplementary

but sturdy

This small volume is the ideal dictionary for typists. It is fully up to date and includes a wealth of classified informaton specially selected for office reference. The print is clear. The price is low. Buy your copy TODAY!

Its size is just right for the office drawer or the handbag.

1 I am 37 years old and my sons are 7 and 3. My father is 73.

2 In only 3 weeks I read 7 books ranging from 77 to 337 pages.

3 My lucky numbers are 3 and 7. My birthday is 3 July, and I am happy when the year has a 3 or a 7 in it. If possible, I always choose a raffle ticket like 33, 77, 37 or 73. When I moved to 77 High Street with its telephone number 73377, I felt my luck was in.

1 For a party of 8, we used 4 bottles of wine and 4 of sherry.

2 The new school will have 488 boys and 448 girls in 48 forms.

3 Consecutive numbers are those which follow one after another, like 3 and 4, or 7 and 8; 37 and 38, or 47 and 48. The larger the numbers, the greater is the risk of confusion: 8,447 and 8,448 or 8,847 and 8,848.

1 I left school at only 16: 6 years later, aged 22, I married.

2 If 12 bring 12 and 12 bring 6, we shall have the 216 needed.

3 In typing numbers, a single error can be critical. A letter sent to 126 instead of 216 Orchard Road could get lost. A reference quoted as 2136 instead of 2316 or a phone number given as 21624 instead of 21264 would be useless. In a business document, a mistype of 26,482 for 26,842 could be serious.

1 The 9 firms had 590 employees, 90 skilled and 500 unskilled.

2 His farm had 950 acres of wheat, 95 of oats and 5 of barley.

3 Very great care should be taken in typing all figures, and they should always be checked. Make this a habit with the small numbers which occur most often, like 5, 9, 10, 12 and 25. Then you are less likely to make mistakes with the larger numbers of 3 or more digits: 590, 950, 1,255, or 5,763 for instance.

Drill:
shift keys

Aunt Sally and Uncle Henry have invited Clare and Betty to Grange Farm in May or June. In October they are going to France where they will visit Paris, Rouen and Deauville.

1 Type the following form on A4 paper.

MIDLANDS DEVELOPMENTS LTD

Residential Developers and
Builders since 1933

Registered office:

Wakeham House
33-36 Kings Road
COVENTRY   CV9 3EM

Telephone: 0203 36939

Q U O T A T I O N / F I N A L   A C C O U N T

No:

Date:

Name:

Work to be carried out/carried out at:

(leave one inch here (6 lines of space))

Job specification:

(leave three inches space here)

For the sum of:

2 *(Complete the form for despatch today)*

Quotation No: 3269 for Mr S Wilson for work to be carried out at 112 London Rd, Cov CV3 9EW

Job specification: Remove brick wall between lounge & dining room. Make good & plaster as necessary. Paint ceiling and walls of new through-room w 2 coats of Dulux white emulsion paint.

For the sum of £650 net.

(Typist - make deletions as appropriate)

Open and full punctuation

1 *Full punctuation* (also known as traditional or standard punctuation) means fully punctuating matter in the traditional style.

2 *Open punctuation* follows the present trend of keeping all punctuation in typewriting to a minimum, in line with the general aim of speeding up and simplifying the work of typists.

Open punctuation therefore means omitting punctuation that does not help make the meaning any clearer. For example, where items are already distinguished by standing on separate lines (in names and addresses, and stock phrases like Dear Sir and Yours truly); or where, as in dates, the meaning is beyond question (4 July 1980); or in abbreviations which are as well (or better) known as their fully spelt-out form (Ltd, OBE)— there is just no need of commas and stops. So they are left out.

However, where punctuation makes the sense clearer and avoids ambiguity, it should not be omitted.

Open punctuation goes well with blocked paragraphs— which again are simpler and faster for the typist, since they do not involve the use of the tabulator. There is, however, no rule that either method of punctuation must be used with any particular style of paragraph.

In this book, open punctuation is used in all typewriting work. In Technique Section 12B on page 57 there is a description of open punctuation as applied to the typing of letters.

Typing abbreviations

An important application of open punctuation is the omission of the full stop after abbreviations. The following examples illustrate this. Note carefully the spacing. The sentences are also given with full punctuation, for comparison.

Open punctuation	*Full punctuation*
a Please come at 7 pm <u>not</u> 8 pm.	Please come at 7 p.m. <u>not</u> 8 p.m.
b Mr T S Waters BSc works here.	Mr. T. S. Waters, B.Sc., works here.
c PS I flew on an MEA plane.	P.S. I flew on an M.E.A. plane.
d Ann is a BBC announcer.	Ann is a B.B.C. announcer.
e Pets, eg dogs and cats, are banned.	Pets, e.g. dogs and cats, are banned.
f NB Raincoats, etc, are needed.	N.B. Raincoats, etc., are needed.
g Augustus ruled from 31 BC to 14 AD.	Augustus ruled from 31 B.C. to 14 A.D.
h A Scot, viz Ian Bell, won the title.	A Scot, viz. Ian Bell, won the title.

The same treatment applies to other recognized abbreviations, like qv, ie, etc, which are always typed and printed in their abbreviated form. They should not be confused with 'drafting' abbreviations (such as *wd* for *would*) which must always be typed in full (*see* pages 34 and 46).

A lazy mind cannot begin to enjoy even the best of Keats' poetry or appreciate the qualities for which it excels.

1   On A4 paper, type the following enrolment form in treble spacing, taking one carbon copy. Leave nine lines of space above the main heading, which should be centred.

Elite: left margin 12; end final dots at 88 on paper scales; tab stop at 75 to start typing *(Mr/Mrs/Miss); tab stop at 48 to start typing Nationality, etc.

Pica: left margin 10; end dots 72; tab stop 59 for *(Mr/Mrs/Miss); tab stop 46 for Nationality, etc.

ENROLMENT FORM

Surname .... *(Mr/Mrs/Miss)

First Name(s) ....

Address ....

....

....

Date of Birth .... Nationality ....

Subject of Course .... (*Elementary)
                                   Intermediate)
                                   Advanced   )

Course Code Number ....

add 1 extra line here

State Day/Evening classes)
and days required   ) ....
                           ....

I enclose cheque/postal order* for £ ....

Signed .... Date ....

* Delete as appropriate

---

2   Complete your two copies of the enrolment form with the two sets of particulars below.

a   Miss Joan Collins of 69 Woodland Avenue, LEEDS LS2 3PS, who was born on 22 May 1965 and is British, wishes to enrol for a course in Intermediate Typewriting. The Course Code Number is T 23 and Joan Collins wants to attend evening classes on Mondays and Thursdays. A cheque for £18.50 is enclosed. Use today's date.

b   Mr John Edward Kramer of 29 Woolgrove Road, LEEDS LS3 4AZ who was born on 12 January 1958 and is American, wishes to enrol for a course in Advanced German. The Course Code Number is G12 and Mr Kramer wishes to attend day classes on Tuesdays and Fridays. A cheque for £27·75 is enclosed.   Use today's date.

3   Repeat tasks 1 and 2 above but this time use spaces (instead of dots) for the insertion of details. Follow each heading with a colon (eg Surname:).

Revise alphabet

1   In his quest for a life of adventure, John met with hazards of every kind, but none more exciting than the perils of mountain-climbing.

Open punctuation and typing abbreviations

2   Open punctuation and the typing of abbreviations are explained in Technique Section 4 on page 31.
Carefully copy—at least twice—each of the sentences (*a* to *h*) using open punctuation.

Blocked paragraphs (figures and abbreviations)

3   For many good reasons it suits some people to start and finish work early, while others prefer later hours. Some offices are able to meet these wishes by arranging for part of the staff to attend - say - from 9 am to 5 pm and the rest from 10 am to 6 pm.

4   In the last paragraph the evening times are given as 5 pm and 6 pm. Some people would like to go over completely to the 24-hour clock. These times would then be expressed as 1700 hrs and 1800 hrs. One instance where the 24-hour clock has been generally adopted is in rail, sea and air passage time-tables.

Indented paragraphs

5   While learning to type, you are working with language. This gives you an opportunity to improve your English - expression, spelling and punctuation. In your own writing, aim to be clear and concise. When copying, look up in a dictionary every new word. Keep your own Vocabulary List of new words with their spelling and meaning and an example of their use.

6   Many typists are not sure when to use figures or words for numbers. In the past there were many rules - so difficult and full of exceptions that few people really grasped them.

        An acceptable guide and working method today is to type all numbers as figures with the following exceptions. Use words for numbers at the start of a sentence and for the number one standing alone. Note, however, that the number one, on its own, should be typed as a figure if it forms part of a group or list of figures: see Unit 14, lines 1 and 2. Observe how the number one is typed in the present paragraph.

SI 1.24

S/A 9 (1 minute)

7   The wet summer spoiled the grain harvest but produced a rich crop of grass for cattle feed.

| 1| 2| 3| 4| 5| 6| 7| 8| 9| 10| 11| 12|

a b c d e f g h i j k l m n o p q r s t u v w x y z

1 On plain A5 portrait paper, type the following tele-phone message sheet in treble spacing, with one carbon copy. Leave nine lines of space above the top heading. Type the last line 2.5 cm (or 1 in) from the bottom of the paper. With a pencil, lightly make a short horizontal mark (erase it later) in the left-hand margin as a guide to assist you in doing this.

Elite: left margin 6; end final dots at 64 on the paper scales;
tab stop at 39—position to start typing date, etc.
Pica: left margin 5; end final dots at 54;
tab stop at 32—position to start typing date, etc.

```
                    TELEPHONE MESSAGE


         Call for ................. Date ............


         Caller ................... Time ............


         ......................... Tel No ..........


         .........................


         Message




         Call taken by ...............................
```

2 Complete each of your copies of the telephone message sheet in turn. Use the following particulars and insert the date of typing.

a Call for Mr T Jackson at 1045 hrs from Mr Holt of Broadway Motors, tele-phone number Crosstown 2486. Your car repairs are now complete. It was found that the tyre of the spare wheel is not roadworthy. Do you want a new tyre fitted on the front offside (where the tyre is worn) and the spare tyre re-placed with this old one? Please telephone him.

b

Call for Mr J Roberts at 1430 hrs from Mr John Williams of Redford Timber Mills. They can at present supply only half the quantity of hardboard that you enquired about yesterday. The earliest they could offer the remainder is in 6 weeks' time. The price would then be higher, but the current price might apply to a firm order now. Telephone him on 01-697 4506.

3 Repeat tasks **1** and **2** above but this time use spaces (instead of dots) for the insertion of details. Follow each heading with a colon (eg Call for:).

The symbols and signs on the figure row differ in position on different keyboards. Always use the appropriate figure finger (otherwise the nearer little finger).

Apostrophe   Remember to practise the finger movement before starting to use the apostrophe in no 2. The main uses of the apostrophe are to show possession or the omission of a letter, as in no 2. Carefully note the spacing when copying. The apostrophe (single quotation mark) is also used as an alternative to double quotation marks—as in no 6.

Question mark   Find the question mark on your typewriter and practise the movement before starting to use it in no 3. The question mark is followed by two spaces at the end of a sentence.

@ **Sign**   Practise the finger movement as usual before starting to type @ in no 4. This sign has limited uses. It should be used only in invoices, statements and similar documents; or in lists of items with prices, as in no 4.

Typing from manuscript   Read through the whole manuscript paragraph (no 5) before starting to type it. Make sure you can read all the words.

Alphabetic sentence

1   A keen and exciting quiz-game was played on television by housewives from Jersey.

' (apostrophe) ●
use shift key

2   John's sister, Mary, is Vera's best friend. They are both in Mr Smith's class at Henderson's School. They couldn't join the school's athletics club last year because they weren't old enough.

? ●
use shift key

3   What is the time? Where shall we go? Shall we walk or take the bus? Shall we be back by tea-time? If not, at what time shall we be back?

@ ●
use shift key

4   The account was made up as follows: 7 newspapers @ 15p each, 4 magazines @ 50p each, and 3 booklets @ 85p each. I hope you will find this correct.

Copy line by line ●

5   *I am writing to ask whether you received my letter which I sent at the end of last month. I am rather concerned as I have heard nothing from you, but the cheque I enclosed has gone through my bank account. I should be glad to receive an early reply.*

Use keys learned

6   Miss Taylor decided that her Christmas purchases should all be 'small in size but good in quality'. As a start she therefore placed the following order: 20 boxes of chocolates @ 95p each; 15 jars of preserved ginger @ 85p each; 6 tins of nuts @ 73p each; and 24 special greetings-cards @ 45p each.

SI 1.26

S/A 10 (1 minute)

7   We should be pleased to receive an early reply to the letter we sent to you early in March.

| 1| 2| 3| 4| 5| 6| 7| 8| 9| 10| 11| 12|

(Additional material on page 38)

UNIT 17   ?   @   Simple manuscript   **33**

It was not just adventure but equally the quest for knowledge that led explorers to face the grim hazards of the Arctic.

1 Type the following form letter on A5 portrait paper, taking two carbon copies. The ringed figures show the number of lines of space to leave. Use margins of 1.5 cm (or ½ in); double spacing for the body of the letter.

SOUTHERN APPLIANCES LIMITED
28-30 The Broadway
LONDON   N8 2AX
①
Telephone 01-770 4321
_____

②
Date:

⑧

Dear

AGREEMENT NO ....

Under the above agreement, we have arranged for our

engineer to call and service/check your heating unit

on ....

at .... If this arrangement is not

convenient, will you please telephone us within 3

days of receipt of this letter.

Yours faithfully

2 Complete each of your three copies of the letter in turn, using the following details and today's date. Insert the inside name and address between the date and the salutation.
a Mrs F Andrews, 21 Long Walk, SOUTHAMPTON SO6 2PS. Agreement No A 4827 79. Heating unit to be serviced (delete 'check' with the typewriter) next Tuesday (give date) at 1000 hrs.
b D Greening Esq, 194 Highgate Hill, ROCHESTER, Kent ME2 5AS. Agreement No G 1745 80. Heating unit to be checked next Wednesday (give date) at 1500 hrs.
c Miss B Light, 96 Wellington Road, CIRENCESTER CO2 3AN. Agreement No L 7934 81. Heating unit to be serviced next Friday (give date) at 1400 hrs.

3 Repeat tasks 1 and 2 above but this time use spaces (instead of dots) for the insertion of details.

Revise ' ? @

1 Didn't you know? Mary's Store has Conrad's cornflakes @ 75p a packet. Isn't that good value?

/ ●
Use shift key

2 We have moved from 20/22 Park Lane to 36/38 Duke Street. Please send all correspondence to the new address.

& ●
Use shift key

3 Mr & Mrs J Williams manage the firm of Williams & Freeman. They considered the premises vacated by Robinson & Marley at 24 & 26 Market Street, but these were unsuitable. However, Walker & Hill moved out of town at just that time. Their premises suited Williams & Freeman admirably.

" ●
Use shift key

4 "Quotation marks", said the teacher, "are easy to use if you just think about their purpose. They enclose direct speech." After a moment's thought the pupil replied, "Yes, but how can I always be sure what is direct speech?"

"The rule", replied the teacher, "is to ask yourself whether the words are quoted exactly as they were spoken. That is direct speech."

Copy line by line ●
Abbreviations in full

5 I am returning the goods under sep. cover + shd be glad to receive suitable replacements by the end of Dec at the latest. If this is not possible, please return my cheque without delay.

Use keys learned

6   The new clerk in Jones & Crocker's of 97/102 Town-end Street is a zealous and helpful young man. Although still only 23 years old, he is making rapid headway in the firm. "Why should not the public expect a square deal?" he asks. Certainly, I was very pleased when he sent my bill for the following: a dinner-set of 48 pieces @ 96p per item; 2 vases @ 85p each; and a teapot @ 93p.

SI 1.26

S/A 11 (1 minute)

7 People with indoor jobs should try to make it a rule to take exercise in the open each day.

| | 1| | 2| | 3| | 4| | 5| | 6| | 7| | 8| | 9| | 10| | 11| | 12| |

(Additional material on page 38)

Drill:

carriage return

(really speed it up)

```
We
We hope
We hope the
We hope the goods
We hope the goods will
We hope the goods will come
We hope the goods will come soon.
```

1 *Technique Section 18 (page 90)*

2 Type the following list of committee members (with lines of dots) on A5 landscape, taking one carbon copy. (With manual typewriters, use a very light touch for the dotted lines.)

Elite: clear any existing tab stops;
       set left-hand margin stop at 20;
       set a tab stop at 44 to establish the point to begin typing the dotted lines;
       make each line of dots 7.5 cm (or 3 in) long (12 dots to 2.5 cm as with any other character);
       begin typing on the eleventh line from the top of the page;
       use vertical spacing shown by the ringed figures.
Pica: as for elite, but left-hand margin at 14, tab stop at 38 (10 dots to 2.5 cm).

```
COMMITTEE
  ②

Lady Atkinson-Barton    ................................
  ①
Dame Edna Lawson        ................................
  ①
Mrs D Millhouse         ................................
  ①
Sir William Tring       ................................
  ①
Miss P Weston           ................................
  ①
Mr A G Windsor          ................................
```

3 Practise paper handling and typing on lines

a Remove your completed list of committee members from the typewriter.
b Re-insert your top copy into the machine and, over the first line of dots, type the first name. Begin typing two spaces to the right of the first dot.
c Remove your paper from the typewriter.
d Re-insert the paper and type the second name over the second line of dots, beginning the name at the same point as the first one.

e Repeat the procedure until you have typed all six names in the list. It is important that you remove your paper after typing each name—to give you plenty of practice in aligning.

Then repeat the task, using the carbon copy you made in task 2. (Time yourself from start to finish.)

Where there are alternative ways of typing money in continuous matter, it is important that the same style be used within a single piece of work.

1 General points

a The £ symbol and p as an abbreviation for pence should never be followed by a full stop—except at the end of a sentence.
b The decimal point is typed as the full stop in its normal position on the line. There must always be two figures after the decimal point to avoid confusion between sums like £24.08—(8p); and £24.80—(80p).
c The £ symbol and the pence abbreviation should never both be included in a single money expression: £25.88; 96p.
d An amount of money represented as figures should not be divided at the end of a line of typing.

2 Pounds only
Any sum comprising pounds only can be typed with or without the decimal point, eg £10.00, £50.00 (or £10, £50). Such round sums can also be given in words (ten pounds, five hundred pounds). Thousands of pounds can be shown as £14,000 or £14 000 (ie with a space instead of a comma).

3 Pence only
Amounts under £1 can be typed with or without the £ symbol and decimal point.

a When *not* using the £ symbol, the pence can be shown either with the word pence typed in full or with the abbreviation p: 25 pence, 77 pence; 25p, 77p. With the *word* pence, the number can be typed as a figure or word: 25 pence or twenty-five pence.
b If the £ symbol were used, the two examples immediately above would appear as £0.25 and £0.77.

4 Mixed amounts, pounds and pence
Any sum over £1 that includes pence is shown as a decimal, eg £10.25 and £500.70.

5 Millions of pounds
Such sums can be shown in various ways:

```
a  It amounts to £3 million but this is a low estimate.
b  It amounts to three million pounds . . .
c  It amounts to £3,000,000 but . . .
d  It amounts to £3 000 000 but . . .
e  It amounts to £3m but . . .
```

Typing measurements in continuous matter

1 One space is left between the number and unit of measurement (see 3 and 4, below).
2 Do not use full stops after abbreviations of measurements.
3 Abbreviations do not take an s in the plural, eg 4 kg, 6 mm, 20 yd, 22 km.
4 An x can be used instead of the word 'by' in measurements. There should be one space before and after the x:

```
The carpet measured 15 m x 12 m and was perfect.
```

5 Figures and measurements should not be divided at the end of lines.

Forms

The technique of form-filling Filling in forms well with a typewriter is easy once a few basic techniques and principles have been mastered.

The *principles* follow what you learned about display. Use the available space to give the typed information a pleasing and well ordered appearance. The *technique* is essentially the ability to move the printing point quickly to any required position on the page. For back and forward movement across the paper, it is generally quicker to use a carriage release lever than to tap the space bar. For rapid movement up and down the page, a cylinder turning knob should be used. To pinpoint quickly the position to begin typing, skilful use of the alignment scale and variable line-spacer or interliner is necessary.

Typing over lines The type, including the lower part of the letters like g p q, should be just clear of the line below it. It is less legible and less pleasing to the eye if it rests on the line. The type should never be allowed to cut through the line. At the other extreme, it should not 'fly in the air' way above the line.

Use the alignment scale, and by means of the variable line-spacer, adjust the paper so that this scale just clears the line you will type on.

Typing in a space

1 When inserting the name and address at the head of the form letter in Unit 44 (between the date and the salutation) you must count how many lines it will take. Then you can work out how many lines of space to leave before starting to type (so that equal space appears above and below).

2 When carrying out Task 3 in Units 44–46, and in working Unit 47, you will in some cases need to insert matter alongside a typed word(s) on the form.

First line up the alignment scale with the bottom of the related type—so that both sets of type will appear exactly in line. You should always leave at least two character spaces before inserting the matter required.

3 When inserting such details as a message (Unit 45) or an address (Unit 46, 47) where possible begin all lines at the same point for neatness and clarity.

Deletions on printed forms Forms often state *Delete as appropriate*. To do this, line up the bottom of the print with the alignment scale and use capital x to strike through any unwanted words.

Footnotes

The asterisks used in Unit 46 are a simple form of footnote. You will also use footnotes in Unit 57 (Simple tabulation).

1 **Footnote signs** Where there are not more than 3 footnotes on a page the signs asterisk *, dagger †, and double dagger ‡ (see page 88) can be used. However, numbers are often preferred—and must be used if a page contains more than three footnotes.

2 **Indicating and typing footnotes** The footnote sign/number is raised *in the text* with no space between it and the word it follows. *At the foot of the typescript/page* at least one line of space is left before the footnote begins. The footnote sign/number is typed in its normal position on the line, at the left-hand margin, with one character space between the sign/number and the footnote itself. Where lengthy, the footnote runs the full length of the typing line, blocked in single spacing. One line of space is left between successive footnotes. Sometimes footnotes are separated from the text above by a line of underscore running from margin to margin: at least one line of space should be left above and below this line.

The typing of money and measurements in continuous matter is explained in Technique Section 5 on page 35.
As you study the numbered points, type out the examples given.

Exclamation mark   This is followed by two spaces at the end of a sentence. (Some keyboards have an exclamation mark key.)

Brackets   No space between a bracket and the enclosed matter. One space before a left-hand bracket, one space after a right-hand bracket, unless followed by a punctuation mark.

Amendments to text often need to be incorported by the typist. All such amendments will be clearly indicated. The manuscript paragraph (no 5) shows two such changes.

a   Deletions without replacement text are clearly crossed through to show the wording has been cancelled. (See lines 2 and 4.)
b   Balloon with arrow The 'balloon' contains the added text, and the arrow clearly marks where it should be inserted.

Revise / & "

1   "No," Alan replied.   "Peck & Day moved to 30/32 Brook Lane. Jackson & Phillips went to 65/67 Main Street."

£
use shift key

2   I bought a chair priced £6.50 and a table marked £12.00. With tax and delivery the bill came to £19.98. A special cash-sale discount, however, brought it down to £17.90. I decided not to buy a sideboard reduced from £185.00 to £130.50, despite the big saving of £54.50.

! *Type apostrophe, backspace once, type full stop*

3   Look out! Stand back! Beware of the dog! Mind the step, Mrs Martin! How clever! Oh, thank you!

( ) *use shift key*

4   The abbreviations (which represent both singular and plural) for some common metric measurements are (in brackets): metre (m), kilometre (km), centimetre (cm), millimetre (mm), gramme (g), kilogramme (kg).

Copy line by line

5   Typing from manuscript makes you realise the importance of good handwriting. Most people do can write clearly if they take a little trouble; and when drafting for typing they must write clearly — if the typist is to make any sense of it! In all manuscript work spelling, too, is important for difficult and uncommon words may not always be fully legible. Are you remembering your Vocabulary List?   (at all)

Use keys learned

6   John Allan and Fred Zimmerman decided to go into business together in the retail trade. The necessary Partnership Deed under the Companies Act was drawn up. (A "partnership" differs from a "private company", whose members have limited liability but whose accounts must be made public.)

SI 1.04

S/A 12 (1 minute)

7   Thank you for your letter in which you asked us to send more chairs. We will see they reach you by the end of next week.

| 1| 2| 3| 4| 5| 6| 7| 8| 9| 10| 11| 12|

(Additional material on page 38)

a b c d e f g h i j k l m n o p q r s t u v w x y z

1 *Technique Section 17B (page 88)*

Practise typing the characters until you can type them with ease. Type them in the manner described, even if your typewriter has special keys for any of them.

2 Copy the following sentences and paragraphs on A4 paper with margins of 2.5 cm (or 1 in). Use single spacing (double between paragraphs and sections).

a H_2SO_4 is the chemical formula for sulphuric acid.

b John scored 85°/o in the examination against a class average of 60°/o.

c In French the name for Francis is François and for Frances it is Françoise.

d The asterisk (*) is a star-shaped mark. The name indeed means 'star', and the character is sometimes called simply a star.

e When we say a place is 30° 25' N and 16° 55' W, we are describing its position in accordance with the lines of latitude and longitude on the world map.

f There are 60 minutes in a degree and 60 seconds in a minute. In very precise measurement, therefore, we might have an angle of 61° 24' 55", read as 61 degrees, 24 minutes, 55 seconds.

g In type, the dagger (†) may not look very much like the weapon it is named after - but in print it does. The double dagger (‡) on the other hand is no more dagger-like in print than in type. Look up dagger and double dagger in a good dictionary to see what they look like in print.

h The following formulae are used to convert temperatures from Fahrenheit to Centigrade (Celsius) and vice versa.

(Take 5/9 of the Fahrenheit number less 32.
(
(Thus 77 ^{o}F = 5/9 x (77 - 32) = 5/9 x 45 = 25 ^{o}C.

(Take 9/5 of the Centigrade number and then add 32.
(
(Thus 25 ^{o}C = (9/5 x 25) + 32 = 45 + 32 = 77 ^{o}F.

i Square brackets are much used in mathematical problems, where brackets within brackets often occur. Elsewhere they separate sharply from the context, words or passages that are interposed in it. Take this example.

The newspaper wrote that last winter was the coldest ever
/this was not borne out by the records/ but less damage
was done than in other recent years.

Here the square brackets show that the enclosed words were not part of the newspaper report, but were added by the writer reporting on it. Ordinary round brackets would not show this so clearly.

Shift lock (the key just above the left-hand shift key) Use this to type consecutive capital letters/upper-case characters.

a Depress shift lock using little finger of left hand.
b Return the left hand to the keyboard and type the capital letters.
c Release shift lock by depressing either left or right shift key.

Underscore

a When underscoring a short word, backspace once for each letter before underscoring.
b When underscoring a long word or several consecutive words, use a carriage release lever to move the car-riage back to start underscoring. Use the shift lock.
c It is considered better practice not to underscore a final punctuation mark. (Some modern typewriters have an automatic underscore facility.)

Correction signs (no 4)

a ⊘ means 'leave as it was'. The writer changed his mind, so type the crossed-out word that has a broken line under it.
b ⌐ means begin a new paragraph.
c ∽ means reverse the order.

Revise £ ! ( )

1 I've found £20 I didn't know I had! I'll give little Annie
£5.50 (for toys) and put the other £14.50 towards a good
night out!

Shift lock ●

2 Much United Nations work is done through the UN Specialised
Agencies. UNICEF is the International Children's Fund.
UNESCO deals with Education; ILO with Labour; WHO with
Health; and UNRRA with Refugees.

Underscore ●
use shift key

3 Efficiency can benefit from division of labour: 'Jack-of-
all-trades is master of none'. Yet too much specialisation
has drawbacks also. The aim should be to find the right
balance.

Copy line by line ● 4
Abbreviations in full

A typewriter is an expensive as well as a useful piece of
equipment. You can both lengthen its life & produce
better ~~quality~~ work by looking after it ~~properly~~ & carefully.

⌐Dust is perhaps the greatest enemy of the typewriter so
keep it as clean as possible. It will help if you always
cover the typewriter at the end of the day & whenever it
(lengthy) will not be used for a period of time. Also,
regularly remove the front cover of the frame & carefully
brush the dust from all the accessible parts of the machine
with a |long-handled| |soft-bristled| brush.

SI 1.11

S/A 13 (1 minute)

5 As you type, keep your eyes on your book as much as you can.
Do not get into the bad habit of watching your keys or work.

| 1| 2| 3| 4| 5| 6| 7| 8| 9| 10| 11| 12|

(Additional material on page 38)

Raising and lowering the paper

Some combination characters and special signs involve the slight raising or lowering of the typewriting paper. This can be done by using the variable line spacer, interliner or (except with single spacing) the half-spacer.

The *variable line spacer* is situated at the end of the left-hand cylinder turning knob and often takes the form of a convex knob. When it is depressed (or in some cases pulled out), the line-spacer ratchet is released so that the cylinder may be moved smoothly to any required position. After its use, the original typewriting line must be found by using the alignment scale.

The *interliner* is a small lever, usually situated on the left-hand side of the carriage. When pulled forwards, it temporarily releases the cylinder from the line-space ratchet so that the cylinder may be moved smoothly to any required position. When the lever is re-engaged, the cylinder returns to the original typing line.

The *half-spacer* When a cylinder turning knob is turned slowly, each 'click' indicates a half-space movement of the cylinder.

Combination characters and special signs
(involving raising/lowering the paper)

Asterisk   Lower the paper slightly, type a small x, backspace once and type a hyphen. On many typewriters the asterisk is provided on the top row of keys.

Brace   Type the left or right bracket sign—whichever is required—one under the other.

Cedilla   Type a small c, backspace once, then type a comma slightly below the c. (Often used in French to give the sound of 's' to a 'c'.)

Dagger   Lower the paper slightly, type a capital I, backspace once and type a hyphen.

Degree sign   Lower the paper slightly and type a lower-case o.

Double dagger   Lower the paper slightly and type two capital Is, the second one a little higher than the other.

Equals sign   Type a hyphen, backspace once, then type a second hyphen slightly above the first one. (Most typewriters have an 'equals' key.)

Per cent sign (per hundred)   Lower the paper slightly and type a small o. Return the paper to the normal typing line and type a solidus followed by a further small o. (Most typewriters have a 'per cent' key.)

Per mille sign (per thousand)   Lower the paper slightly and type a small o. Return the paper to the normal typing line and type a solidus followed by two further small o's.

Section mark   Type a small or capital S and backspace once. Then slightly raise the paper and type a second small or capital S.

Square brackets   Type a solidus, backspace once and type an underscore character. Then lower the paper one line space (use the half-spacer twice), and type an underscore. For the right-hand bracket, type a solidus, backspace twice and type an underscore. Then lower the paper one space, and type an underscore.

metals*

(
(
(

garçon

notes‡

15°

query‡

=

24°/o

2°/oo

§ or ş

[ ]

Inferior characters (subscripts)   Any characters typed below the normal typing line.

H_2O CO_2

Chemical symbols.

Superior characters (superscripts)   Any characters typed above the normal typing line. (You will find other examples in the above list.)

$x = a^2 \times b^3$

Algebraic expression.

Unit 17 (new characters ' ? @)	Where should I do mother's shopping? Bell's self-service store in town was better value than Goodman's in the village. Had I time, however, to catch the hourly bus to town? I managed to do so, and bought the following: 2 packets of cereal @ 70p each; 1 carton of cream @ 68p; 3 tins of peaches @ 65p each; and 2 jars of Wilson's marmalade @ 49p each.
Unit 18 (new characters / & ")	Simon & Isaacson have opened a shop at 28/30 Main Street, opposite Newman & Price's at No 49/51. These jewellery firms' rival advertisements now claim "Lowest Prices in Town" and "Value Unbeatable"; or "Best Prices Paid for Old Gold/Silver" and "Top Value for Your Unwanted Jewels". Such keen competition should benefit the public.
Unit 19 (new characters £ ( ) !)	At this cold and dismal time of year, very good holiday terms are on offer. Think of a week in Rome (air travel from London, hotel and meals included) for only £250! Or 2 weeks by the warm sea beaches of Barbados (10 hours flight from London) for £750! There are many other tempting offers.
Unit 20 (shift lock and underscore)	For the sake of clarity, application forms often ask for information in block capitals. Personal names like JAMIESON or GEOGHAN and addresses like 77 THURLOE STREET can be very difficult to read in unfamiliar handwriting. While this does not apply to typescript, block capitals should be used even in typing when so requested.
Carriage return (*really speed it up*)	We We shall We shall send We shall send the We shall send the goods We shall send the goods tomorrow.
Shift keys and comma	Amy, Bob, Con, Dan, Eve, Fred, Gert, Hugh, Ida, Jet, Ken, Liz, Mo, Ned, Olga, Pam, Quin, Rose, Sid, Ted, Una, Vera, Win, Xavier, Yves, Zena.
Phrases	on the, in the, to the, from the, and the, if the, when the, is the, at the, with the, and we shall, if they will, it is, when do you, how can he, what do you, thank you for, we hope
Double letters	kraal, rubber, acclaim, ladder, deed, suffer, egg, fill, hammer, sinner, soon, upper, arrest, kiss, mutter, buzz. Sally-Anne Summers looked in terror at the compass needle.

Wise people who invested in jade and antique boxes found
their money had zoomed in value. Those with money in the
bank found it had lost a great deal of purchasing power.

1 *Technique Section 17A (page 86)*

Practise the examples given in the extreme right-hand column. Make them in
the manner described, even if your typewriter has special keys for any of them.

2 Copy the following sentences and paragraphs on A4 paper with margins of
2.5 cm (or 1 in). Use single spacing (double between paragraphs and sections)

a   What a price! The figure is 3/5 of my monthly salary!

b   The fraction can be expressed as 5 2/5 or 5.40 in decimal
terms.

c   My 4-year-old brother already does sums like 28 x 2 and
93 ÷ 3!

d   In New York I bought for $15.95 a suitcase measuring
2' 6" x 1' 9". This was 95¢ cheaper than the price in
Dallas.

e   In the USA, the dime is a coin worth 1/10 of a dollar
($1), or 10¢. A nickel is a 5¢ piece, originally made
of copper and nickel.

f   Calculate as quickly as you can $3.25 x 15.
"   " "   " " "   97¢ - 68¢.
"   " "   " " "   360' 10" ÷ 4' 5".

g   The dollar sign ($) is thought to come from the Spanish
dollar, or 'piece of eight' (8 reals). The S is
believed to be a broken 8. The Spanish piece of eight
pictured the 2 Pillars of Hercules. This may be the
origin of the 2 bars that cross the S in the dollar sign
in printing.

h   When you come across a new word like 'caret', it is
useful to look it up in a dictionary. You will find
(appropriately) that caret is Latin for 'something is
wanting'. It has nothing to do with the carat that is a
measure of the purity of gold.

'Ditto' also derives from Latin, and means 'it has been
said'. So there is no need to type it all over again!

i   Diaeresis is a difficult word, and like the diaeresis
sign it is now seldom used in the English language. The
purpose of the diaeresis is to show that the second of 2
adjacent vowels is pronounced separately. Thus 'naïve'
has 2 syllables, while 'nail' has only one. This 2-dot
sign occurs over certain vowels in other languages. In
German, known as Umlaut, it has the effect of changing
the vowel sound, as in the place names Düsseldorf and
Münster.

You will now learn how to set and make your own right-hand margin.

1 Line-end bell A 'warning' bell rings on your typewriter about six spaces before you reach the position where the right-hand margin stop is set. The carriage locks at the margin stop position and you can only type beyond it by pressing the margin release key. This is often found at the top right-hand side of the keyboard—but its position varies with different machines.

2 Check these two points on your typewriter

a Find out the number of letters or spaces you can type after the warning bell before the carriage locks. Lightly type consecutive full stops when doing this.
b Find the position of your margin release key and check how it works.

3 Making your own right-hand margin In normal typing, the right-hand margin cannot be as even as the left one, but you will want to keep your margin as even as possible—as close as you can to the point where you set the margin stop. Often you will finish the line a space or two before the margin position; likewise, you will sometimes type a space or two beyond the margin position (by using the margin release key).

In the modern trend, many skilled typists never divide words at the end of lines, yet manage to achieve a satisfactorily even right-hand margin to their work. This way they avoid having to give frequent attention to the somewhat complex rules for line-end division of words. And they avoid wasting time. It is recommended that you follow their example. However, there may be occasions when you feel that word division is desirable, so the 'rules' are stated here for you to study. When you have read them through, you will appreciate even more the merits of not dividing!

Use of hyphen When you divide a word at the end of a line, you must use a hyphen. The hyphen should always be typed at the *end* of the line—never carried over to the beginning of the following line.

4 Guidelines for word division

a The *pronunciation* of a word is the first factor to consider and several of the following rules are covered by this point. In general, the typist should divide between syllables. This will be clear if you say a word aloud and note the way it falls into natural syllables, eg pic-ture, lan-tern. Words should be divided at these natural points.
b Words that begin with a *prefix* are well divided after the prefix, eg con-sider, trans-fer. Likewise, words ending with a *suffix* are well divided before the suffix, eg pain-less, knowledge-able.
c When *double consonants* occur in the middle of a word, divide between them, eg permis-sion, interrogate. However, if a root word ends in a double consonant, the division should be made after the root word, eg miss-ing, tell-ing.
d When *three consonants* come together in the middle of a word, divide according to the consonants that are pronounced together, eg scram-bling, trium-phant.
e Words that *already contain a hyphen* should be divided at the point of the hyphen and never split a second time, eg self-reliant, second-class.
f *Composite words* should be divided into their original parts, eg school-master, mantel-piece.

5 Words should not be divided in the following cases

a Words of one syllable should not be divided, eg brought, crouched.
b Numbers and sets of figures should not be divided, eg £500.65, 14 m × 12 m.
c Abbreviations should not be divided, eg UNESCO, O & M.
d The last word of a paragraph or page is best not divided.
e When division of a word would lead to misunderstanding, eg sip-hon, it should not be divided.

1 Combination characters A combination character is formed from two single characters. Some combination characters are simple to type and involve merely the use of the backspace key; for others the paper must be raised or lowered. In Unit 19 you first typed an exclamation mark. Since this combines the use of two keys—the apostrophe and the full stop—it is a combination character.

2 Special signs A special sign uses a key already on the typewriter, but for a purpose different from its usual one. Use of the full-stop key for the decimal point (which you first typed in Unit 19) is an example of this.

Combination characters and special signs increase the number of symbols a typewriter will produce without adding to the standard number of keys. Your typewriter may have keys for some of them. Even if this is so, practise making the combination characters in the manner described. You may not always be using a machine with special keys.

3 Combination characters and special signs
(not involving raising/lowering the paper)

Caret sign Formed by typing a / (solidus), backspacing once and using the _ (underscore) key. Used to show an omission.

$\angle$

Cent sign Type a small c, backspace once and use the solidus. Used in various currencies.

¢

Decimal point Type the full stop in its normal position.

6.5

Diaeresis (umlaut) Type the required letter, backspace once and type double quotation marks. In English this sign has virtually died out—but it is used in some foreign languages.

Brontë

Ditto sign Use the double quotation marks key. It may be typed under the first letter of each word that is repeated, or under the centre of each word that is repeated.

"

Division sign Type a colon, backspace once and type a hyphen.

÷

Dollar sign Type a capital S, backspace once and type a solidus.

$

Exclamation mark Type an apostrophe, backspace once and type a full stop.

!

Feet or minutes Use the apostrophe key.

12'

Inches or seconds Use double quotation marks.

8"

Minus sign Use a hyphen with a space before and after it.

6 - 2·

Multiplication sign Use a small x with a space before and after it.

6 x 2

Sloping fractions Use the solidus. One space should be left after an accompanying whole number. Most typewriters have special keys for commonly-used fractions.

6 3/5

4 Plus sign and accents Where there are no special keys for the plus sign (+) and accents [(´) acute, (`) grave, and (^) circumflex], they cannot be formed satisfactorily on the typewriter. After the paper has been removed from the machine, they should be neatly inserted with a matching-colour ink.

Drill:
alphabetic sentence

A path of crazy paving ran to the extreme end of the garden
where a quick-running stream formed the boundary with the
adjoining farmland.

Technique Section 6 (page 39)

Copy the following passage on a sheet of A4 paper, with indented paragraphs as shown. Begin typing on the tenth line down from the top of the page. (Insert the paper and adjust it so that its top edge lines up with the top of the alignment scale—the scale on the two plastic shields either side of the printing point—and use the carriage return ten times in single spacing.)
Type the passage in double spacing (line space selec-

tor at 2) and set your margins as follows:

elite—18 left, 85 right
pica—15 left, 70 right

Make your own right-hand margin, keeping it as even as possible. Weigh up the position each time your line-end bell rings. If you are not satisfied with your first attempt, copy the passage a second time.

My friend, Freda, is a great one for auction sales. She says she gets

more fun and pleasure out of them than going to the cinema. Anyway, she

hasn't much money left for cinema-going after getting carried away at an

auction! They have a certain atmosphere and excitement that make them

irresistible: or so she says.

On one occasion Freda persuaded me to attend an auction held in the

local mansion (whose owner had gone bankrupt). I arrived a little late and

when she saw me enter the door she waved her catalogue in greeting.

Unfortunately for Freda, this gesture was made at a crucial moment in the

proceedings - and she found herself the reluctant owner of an elegant but

somewhat tatty and worm-eaten sofa!

However, it was bonfire week so we put it on her son's bonfire and

shared both the cost and the enjoyment. The sofa certainly helped make a

marvellous fire - and as I munched my sausages, I sadly reflected on its

former glory as it descended and melted in the centre of the flames.

SI 1.16

S/A 14 (1 minute)

We shall send you a cheque for the china just as soon as you
replace the broken plates that we returned to you last week.

| 1| 2| 3| 4| 5| 6| 7| 8| 9| 10| 11| 12|

Date	No of Timing	Length of Timing	Gross Speed wpm	Net Controlled Speed wpm
30 September	3	3 mins	35	28
2 October	4	4 mins	36	30

7 Setting your goal for net controlled speed   At the start of the three-minute S/A timings, set yourself a goal for net controlled speed in the three-minute passages. A suggestion is to pitch your goal at the highest forced speed you achieved in any of the last three of your two-minute timings.

Practise, in turn, the three-minute passages, in a cyclic manner until you have reached your goal in each passage. Each time you achieve your goal, ring it in the net controlled speed column of your form.

8 Progressing from 3-minute to 4-minute passages and timings   Only when this goal has been achieved should you move on to four-minute timings. You should then set yourself a higher speed goal for net controlled speed; base it on your highest forced speed in the last of the three-minute timings. The four-minute passages should again be taken in a cyclic manner and you should not proceed to the five-minute passages until you have achieved your speed/accuracy goal on each of the four-minute ones.

9 Typing the S/A passages   You will find it convenient to use blocked paragraphs and to follow the line endings given where the passages are typed to a 60-stroke line. Do *not* correct your errors.

Although typing in single spacing is economical in the use of paper, it is trying to the eyes when a lengthy passage has to be carefully checked for errors: therefore you may prefer to use 1½ or double spacing. If you finish typing a passage before the timing is up, start it a second time.

10 Syllabic intensity (*see also page 17*)   You are familiar with syllabic intensity and will have noted that it has been stated for all the S/A passages you have typed. All the S/A passages from now on are in the SI range 1.35–1.41, generally considered within the 'average difficulty' level. The SI is assessed over each 50 words—since the longer and more difficult words should be spread evenly throughout the passage.

11 Realize your speed potential   The aim of the S/A work in this course is that everyone should attain his/her highest speed combined with accuracy. The permitted error tolerance deals with the accuracy aspect; in time, as you become more expert, you may set yourself even higher standards in this respect. For the present, provided the accuracy standard given here is observed, let your high-speed potential be developed. Bear in mind that it is by improving on your own previous best that you will successfully develop your own potential to the full.

Half-space correction

This is a useful method of substituting a correct word for a wrong one within a typed passage, provided the new word has only one character more, or less, than the one to be replaced—eg 'have' for 'has' or vice versa. Half-space correction can avoid the need for retyping of the typescript. There are several ways of half-space correcting, but the easiest and most reliable is as follows. First erase the incorrect word in full. Then, *if the new word is one character longer*, move the carriage to the position where the second letter of the old word was typed. At that point, hold the backspace key right down, type the first letter of the new word, and release the backspace key. Then tap one space. Again hold down the backspace key, type the second letter and release

the backspace key. Deal with each subsequent letter in the same way. The new word will appear with half a character space, instead of a full one, on either side.

If the new word is one character shorter than the old one, the procedure is the same except that the carriage should be moved at the start to the position where the third letter of the old word was typed. The new word will appear with one-and-a-half character spaces on either side.

In both cases, the slight variation from the normal space between words is scarcely noticeable. Most typewriting examiners accept half-space correction, if it is well done, without penalty. Some typewriters (especially electrics) have a special half-space key.

TECHNIQUE 16 Speed/accuracy development
(3, 4, 5-minute timings)
Half-space correction
85

From now on, as soon as you realize you have made a mistake, correct it. With manual methods you will find it takes time and patience to correct well—but you will become even more aware of the need for good, accurate typing.

It is much easier to correct work while the paper is still in the typewriter, so make a habit of checking each page of typewritten work before removing it from the machine.

1 Use of a rubber typewriter eraser

a Lift the paper bail out of the way.
b With a cylinder-turning knob, raise the paper so that the error lies above the erasure table (the sloping metal bar immediately above the cylinder).
c Move the carriage to the extreme right or left position (whichever is nearer the error) using the margin release key in conjunction with a carriage release leaver. This will prevent eraser particles from falling into the type basket (important in the care of your machine).
d Carefully remove the ink of the error, first with a soft rubber and finally with a hard one, using a gentle, up-and-down motion. Rub only on the error. Keep your fingers away from the paper to avoid smudging.
e Firmly brush or blow away from the typewriter any eraser particles.
f Return to the same line and position as the error.
g Replace the paper bail.
h Type in the correction—making sure (with manual typewriters) that you use normal pressure on the key(s) so that the error will not 'stand out'.

2 Other methods of correcting
The procedure for locating the error for correction, and returning the carriage for typing, is the same as above.

a **Correction liquid** This is applied with a small brush attached to the stopper of the bottle, like a nail-varnish brush. Various tints are available as well as standard white, and it is necessary to match the liquid with the paper if a good result is to be achieved.

With time the liquid in the bottle tends to thicken and must be kept to an even flowing consistency: special 'thinner' is supplied for this purpose.

The error should be carefully painted over and the correction typed after the liquid has dried. It is important to use the liquid sparingly and to wait until it has completely dried before typing the correction. Otherwise an unsightly smudge will result, also, the liquid will smear the typewriter—particularly on the plastic shields situated either side of the printing point, and on the rubber grips on the paper bail. Great care must, of course, be taken to ensure that the liquid is not spilt from the bottle into the typewriter.

b **Correction paper** This is a specifically-prepared strip of paper, coated on one side with powder, and again in a variety of shades to match the paper. If the faulty character is typed again, through one of these strips, it is blotted out with the powder. The strip is then removed and the correction typed in.

The same spot on the correction strip should not be used more than once, or the error will not be covered. Also, if the page of work is frequently handled or folded, the coating powder tends to wear off, revealing the error and leaving the impression of an overtype.

3 Electric and electronic typewriters
may offer additional methods of correction (consult Instruction Booklet).

a Cover-up correction ribbon feature—works like correction paper.
b Lift-off correction ribbon feature—works only with correctable film ribbon.
c Window display panel—typist corrects error(s) on panel before the text is committed to paper.

4 Correcting after removal from machine

a Remove error with eraser or correction liquid.
b Re-insert the paper into the typewriter.
c Ensure good alignment before typing in the correction. Using the paper release lever, bring a 'thin' letter (eg i or l) exactly above the printing point, and make sure the typing is in line with the alignment scale (see 5). Then use the variable line spacer (see 6) to get the typing line level with the alignment scale.
d Check alignment and position by moving the ribbon position indicator to white (which disengages the ribbon), and lightly tapping a trial first letter.
e If no further adjustment is needed, return ribbon position to blue (or black) and type the correction.

5 Alignment scale
This will be found on the transparent plastic shields either side of the printing point. The alignment scale is a series of vertical marks—the upper tips of which indicate the bottom of the typing line (check your machine for accuracy here).

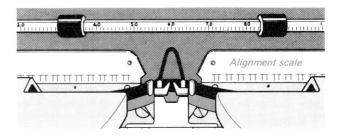

Alignment scale

6 Variable line spacer
This is situated at the outer end of the left cylinder-turning knob. When it is depressed (or in some cases pulled out) the line-space ratchet is released so that the cylinder may be smoothly moved up or down to any required position.

You will now progress to speed/accuracy timings of three minutes (and later of four and five minutes). From now on, the S/A passages will not be included in the units of work. They are longer and will take more time to practise. Therefore they are grouped together at the **end of the book on pages 122 to 125. You should,** however, continue as before with regular practice in speed/accuracy development.

1 **Permitted error tolerance** From this point you must continue to increase the speed at which your fingers work in steps 2 and 3. But you must also adopt a specific standard of accuracy in assessing your work in steps 1 and 4.

Thus there will be (*a*) a *gross speed*, measured by the full extent of your typing in steps 2 and 3; and (*b*) a *net controlled speed* in steps 1 and 4, which will disregard everything typed after the error cut-off point (see 2 below).

The allowance for net controlled speed will be one error per minute of timing, plus one overall. This may seem a high standard at first, and your recorded speeds may suffer a check. It is, however, a realistic standard for line by line copying of this kind. You cannot justifiably talk of your 'speed' unless you can type it with reasonable accuracy.

2 **Applying the error tolerance** The allowance of one error per minute of typing plus one error overall means the following:

a   In a 3-minute timing 4 errors are permitted.
b   In a 4-minute timing 5 errors are permitted.
c   In a 5-minute timing 6 errors are permitted.

In order to assess your net controlled speed, count the words you typed up to and including the word before the 5th error (in a 3-minute timing); 6th error (in a 4-minute timing); 7th error (in a 5-minute timing). In each case this is the *error cut-off point*.

3 **Counting five-stroke standard words** Until now, you have counted each letter/space/character as one stroke towards the standard five-stroke word. From now on, since you are no longer using the five-stroke scale across the bottom of the S/A passage, the examination method of counting can be fully applied. The difference from what you have done before is that you will now add one stroke for each manipulative action—each time you use a shift key, backspace, etc. Thus, a question mark will count as two strokes—one for use of the shift key and one for striking the question mark key.

4 **Counting your speed** In the S/A passages as now presented, you are given at the end of each line the cumulative stroke count up to the end of that line. When your timing is completed, take the stroke count given at the end of the last complete line you typed. Divide this figure by five—to find the number of standard words. Add to that the number of standard words typed in any remaining part-line (counted by the method just described in 3 above). Divide the total number of standard words you typed by the number of minutes in the timing, to find your speed in words per minute. For instance, if you typed 105 standard words in three minutes, your gross speed was 35 wpm. (Make any calculations in the margin.) Your net controlled speed should be counted in the same way, but only to the error cut-off point.

5 **Speed/accuracy timings** Recall now the familiar four-step pattern:

Step 1   Three minutes exactly, typing at your highest *controlled speed* (the highest speed at which you can maintain reasonable accuracy).

Step 2   Three minutes exactly, aiming for *increased speed* even though more errors may occur.

Step 3   Three minutes exactly—a determined drive to *push your speed even higher* (but not to the extent of sacrificing good techniques, with 'wild' key striking).

Step 4   Three minutes exactly, dropping back to your highest *controlled speed.*

When time permits, you should continue to follow this pattern. If time does not allow for all four steps, omit step 3. If time is very short, just use step 1 (remembering to count your speed only to the error cut-off point). For success in S/A training—as in all 'competitive' skills—you should be physically relaxed but mentally alert. The mental concentration required is intense, so do relax completely in the short breaks between timings.

6 **Recording your performance** From now on, you will use the form of record shown on the next page.

In the gross speed column, record the highest speed reached in any of your timings on the S/A passage, regardless of errors. This will normally be in step 3.
In the net controlled speed column, record the highest speed you achieved up to the error cut-off point. This will usually be in step 4, but it might be in one of the other steps, so check your work in each one up to the error cut-off point.

Although quite dazed and shaken, David Young fought on to
win the junior boxing championship.

1 *Technique Section 7 (page 41)*

Type each of the following sentences as it stands. Then make the correction
shown. Use double spacing between sentences.

I do not know where this college is. (*correct 'this' to 'that'*)

John had never felt so happy in his life. (*correct 'had' to 'has'*)

Of all the gardens I have seen, these were the finest. (*correct 'these' to 'those'*)

2 Read through, then copy the following passage on
a new sheet of A4 paper, with indented paragraphs and
in double spacing, as shown. Begin typing on the
tenth line down from the top of the page, as you did in
Unit 21; and use the same margins.

Make your own right-hand margin, keeping it as even
as possible. Carefully correct all errors as you go along.
Give your work a final check through before removing
it from the typewriter. Repeat the task if your copy is
not mailable (or usable).

From now on, you should correct any errors you make. When you first

started to type, you probably made far more mistakes than you do now. If you

made a real effort to put right <u>persistent</u> errors - as you were asked to do

after you typed Unit 11 - you should have seen a marked decrease in your

mistakes. No doubt your typing skill has progressed well since then.

In all your typing in future - unless you are given specific instructions

to the contrary - you should repeat a typing task only if you consider that

your typing is not 'mailable' or 'usable'.

In office work it is important that all typing is of mailable standard.

This means that it should be correctly copied with all errors corrected; and

with all drafting abbreviations typed in full. In addition, your work should

be clean and neat; should show an even 'touch' (with manual typewriters); and

should be pleasingly arranged on the paper.

SI 1.22

You must always think hard when you are typing and make sure
you use the right finger. Copy each word with extreme care.

| 1| 2| 3| 4| 5| 6| 7| 8| 9| 10| 11| 12|

Where do flies go in winter? Ask me another! Don't we all
agree, though, that it's good to be curious (without being
tedious)? A teacher's patience is often strained by "silly"
questions. But doesn't <u>serious</u> questioning show a real
interest in learning? That is <u>always</u> welcome!

1 Type the following passage, using equal side margins and a dropped head.
Centre all headings. Type the figures at the left-hand margin position and leave
two spaces after them, as shown.

KEEPING YOUR TYPEWRITER CLEAN

To produce good typewriting, your machine must be kept clean. Dust
and dirt clog the mechanism, and blur the characters. This can spoil
well-typed work. As with all machines, cleaning should be routine. Here
is a simple procedure to follow regularly. Always keep at hand a cleaning
kit of the materials required.

Daily Routine

1 Cover the machine overnight.

2 Remove the front cover from the frame and carefully brush the dust from
all accessible parts with a long-handled, soft-bristled brush.

 3 Carefully raise the base of the typewriter and dust its underneath parts
and the desk below.

4 Clean the typefaces with a stiff-bristled brush, damped with a drop of
methylated spirit.

Weekly Routine

1 Using a clean, soft duster, remove all dirt and oil from the carriage
rails.

Then lightly apply a little clean typewriter oil. (No other parts
should be oiled by the typist.)

2 Polish all plate work and enamel, using a few drops of spirit on the
duster. Likewise wipe the cylinder.

Typewriter Servicing

Typewriters that are in general use should receive a general service
and cleaning by a mechanic at least every 3 months.

2 Type the above passage a second time: this time use unequal side margins.

SI 1.32

It is truly said that any good typist must be able to spell.
It should be added that anyone keen to be a typist can learn
to spell. Often people who spell badly are not aware of the
fact. So we must test our spelling by watching the words as
we read books and daily newspapers. Practice makes perfect.

| 1| 2| 3| 4| 5| 6| 7| 8| 9| 10| 11| 12|

Carbon paper   In many of your typewriting tasks you will need to take one or more carbon copies. For this you need special paper with a carbon coating on one side and special 'flimsy' paper to take the copy. The carbonized side must face the paper on which the copy is to appear.

Carbon paper is available in a variety of qualities and colours—blue, black, purple, green, red and brown. Black and blue are the most commonly-used colours for general purposes.

Taking one carbon copy   (see illustration below)

1   Place a sheet of flimsy paper on your desk.

2   On top of this, place a sheet of carbon paper of the same size—with the carbonized side facing the flimsy.

3   Then place the paper on which you will type (called 'the top copy') on top of the carbon paper.

4   Pick up the papers together from the bottom, turning them so that the flimsy faces you.

5   Align the papers at the top and on the left by gently tapping them on the desk and carefully manipulating them with the fingers.

6   Then insert the papers into the typewriter, with the flimsy still facing you.

7   If the papers need further aligning, the paper release lever should be used.

Taking more than one carbon copy   The method of arranging the papers before insertion into the typewriter is the same. Place above the first flimsy and carbon sheet as many further flimsies and carbons as are required, before placing the top copy above the last sheet of carbon paper. There is always one sheet more of typing paper than of carbon paper.

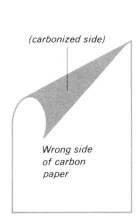

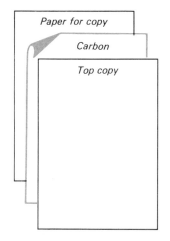

The deep-coloured carbonized side of the paper produces a copy

The carbonized side must face the paper on which the copy will appear

Note three sheets of typing paper, two sheets of carbon paper

Special backing sheet   To make it easier to insert several sheets into the typewriter at once, a special backing sheet with a folded end can be used—to help keep the edges straight and in line.

Points to observe when carbon copying

1   The type faces should be clean and in good condition for the production of clear copies.

2   With manual typewriters use a sharp, even touch. Any unevenness in striking the keys will show up even more on the carbon copies than on the top copy.

Handling and storing carbon paper

1   Carbon paper should be handled lightly and carefully or the carbon deposit will get on the hands, resulting in messy work.

2   Carbon paper should occasionally be turned top to bottom and a narrow strip cut off the top or bottom edge. This will ensure you get maximum use from each carbon sheet by using the carbonized area between the original typing lines.

3   Store carbon paper flat (preferably in a box) away from heat. If carbon paper gets creased or wrinkled, poor copies will result—with a 'treeing' effect.

Erasing when taking a carbon copy

1   Insert a small slip of paper behind the sheet of carbon paper at the point of the error.

2   Erase the error on the top copy in the usual way.

3   Remove the slip of paper and then erase the error on the carbon copy.

Numbers can be divided evenly by 3 if the sum of the digits is divisible by 3 - 309, 678, 2,895, 15,786, 478,674. (In these numbers the digits total 12, 21, 24, 27, 36. Check that yours are correct.) Where, as with the last 2 numbers, the sum of the digits is divisible by 9, the numbers also are divisible by 9.

1 *Technique Sections 15A and 15B (pages 80 and 81)*

2 Copy the following passage on A4 paper, using double spacing and indented paragraphs. Use equal margins and a 'dropped head'. Centre the main heading and sub-heading. Read the passage through before you start typing. It contains important information. (4 ringed errors to correct.)

ESSENTIAL INFORMATION FOR TYPISTS

A Main Heading and a Sub-heading

As in notices and other kinds of display that you have already typed, so within a multi-line heading over continuous typing, the style and line spacing should vary according to the purpose and affect desired.

The lines of the heading should not be too spaced out or they will loose their impact: nor should they be cramped together. Full use should be made of the various devices to give prominence to particular parts of the heading - spaced capitals, closed capitals, initial capitals, underscoring, varying the vertical space, etc. Here the artistic skill of the typist comes into play.

In this piece of typescript there is one line of space between the main and sub-heading and two lines of space between the sub-heading and the start of the first paragraph. the extra line of space above the continuous typing has the dual effect of lending prominence to the headings and giving a more balanced and pleasing appearance to the work .

3 Copy the above passage a second time; this time use unequal margins of 2.5 cm (or 1 in) and 1.5 cm (or ½ in).

SI 1.28

S/A 32 (2 minutes)

The good typist should at all times bear in mind the need to save paper. As with most things, however, there is true and false economy. Good work is never crowded on a page. So be careful in choosing the size of paper and avoid false starts and all rash errors which cause whole pages to be destroyed.

| 1| 2| 3| 4| 5| 6| 7| 8| 9| 10| 11| 12|

Drill:
alphabetic sentence

I enjoyed the dazzling show of the soldiers in their vivid
ceremonial uniforms, but it lacked the expertise of the
sailors' quick-landing drill.

Technique Section 8 (page 43)

Copy the following passage on a sheet of A4 paper, with indented paragraphs
and in double spacing, as shown. Take one carbon copy. Begin typing on the
tenth line down from the top of the page. Use the same margins as in Unit 21.
Make your own right-hand margin, keeping it as even as possible. Carefully
correct any errors as you go along. Repeat the task if your copy is not mailable.

Taking copies with carbon paper is the most widely-used means of

producing 1 or 2 copies of a document. In most offices, at least one carbon

is normally taken of every letter, memo, etc.

In some offices, carbon copies are not taken - a copying machine is

used instead. However, this is a fairly expensive process; and it is not

always possible to have a copying machine readily to hand for all typists to

use. The immediacy and cheapness of carbon copying make this method ideal

for routine typing when only 1 or 2 copies are required.

It is necessary, for reference purposes, for a business to have a copy

of every letter and document it sends out. This should be an exact copy of

the original. Therefore, when you correct your typing errors, remember to

correct carefully the carbon copy as well. A carbon copy should be a legible

and accurate copy of your typing. If it is not, you may find yourself in

trouble!

SI 1.26

S/A 16 (1 minute)

I intend this year to learn to play bridge. My friends tell
me there is no better game for pleasure and memory training.
| 1| 2| 3| 4| 5| 6| 7| 8| 9| 10| 11| 12|

Unequal side margins

In work that contains little or no centring, a left-hand margin of 2.5 cm (or 1 in) and a right-hand margin of 1.5 cm (or ½ in) are commonly used. If you wished to centre with these margins you would need to find the centre point of the typing line and then backspace once for every two characters in the line to be centred.

Unequal margins of 1 inch and ½ inch using elite type:

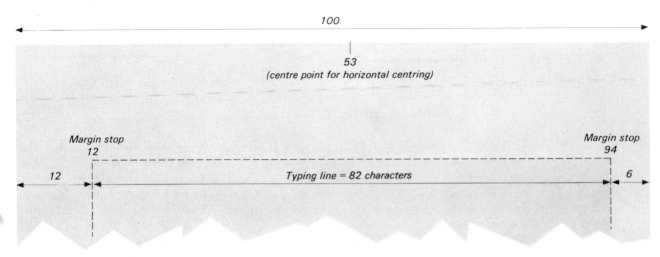

Centre point of typing line:

a Add together the numbers at which the margins are set (12 + 94 = 106).
b Divide the answer by two (106 ÷ 2 = 53). This is the centre of the typing line and the point from which you should backspace when centring horizontally.

Unequal margins of 1 inch and ½ inch using pica type:

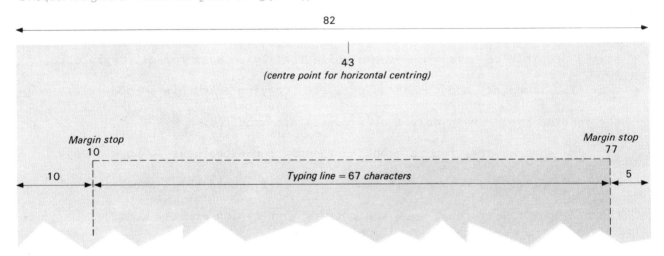

Centre point of typing line:

a Add together the numbers at which the margins are set (10 + 77 = 87).
b Divide the answer by two (87 ÷ 2 = 43½). As always, ignore the fraction and say 43. This is the centre point of the typing line and the point from which you should backspace when centring horizontally.

Note the 'short cut' method When the right and left margins differ by not more than half an inch, establish the centre point of the typing line by adding three to the centre point figure of the paper.

a b c d e f g h i j k l m n o p q r s t u v w x y z

1   On A4 paper type the following passage. Use double spacing and blocked paragraphs. Use the carriage return twice between paragraphs. Type the heading as shown—beginning at the left-hand margin, and leave the two lines of space after it. Start typing on the tenth line down from the top of the paper. No carbon copy required. Repeat this task only if your typing is not of mailable standard. (Two ringed errors to correct.)

Margins: elite — 18 left, 85 right
         pica — 15 left, 70 right

CHANGING YOUR TYPEWRITER RIBBON

When your typewriter ribbon becomes very worn, the typescript will be faint. You ~~will~~ then need to replace the ribbon with a new one. Before you do this make sure, from the explanation below, that both top and bottom of the ribbon have been ~~fully~~ used. [Bichrome ribbons (with one half blank and the other half red) are obviously uneconomical unless the red is needed often. In many offices, plain black ribbons are used so that when the top half becomes worn, the ribbons is changed from one spool to the other to bring the lower half into use.

This half could be brought into use (b y) moving the ribbon position indicator to RED. For speed and ease of typing, however, most typists prefer to turn the ribbon so that the part in use is always at the top.

2   On another sheet of A4 paper, type the following passage. Use the same instructions as in the last task, except that this one requires a carbon copy. Note that at the end of the passage a caret sign ⋏ is used to show where 'quickly' must be inserted. Also, ∥ is used as an alternative to [to show where a new paragraph must begin.

FITTING A NEW RIBBON

Instructions for fitting a new ribbon are given in the Instruction Booklet for your typewriter. If this is not available, note very (and wound) carefully how the ribbon is fitted before removing the old one. This varies considerably with different makes of typewriter: to give but one example - on some machines the ribbon approaches the spool from the back and on others from the front. It is usually easier to thread a new ribbon at the printing point if the shift lock is engaged, as this gives better access to the ribbon vibrator. ∥Many modern type-writers have a ribbon cassette system. The cassette enclosing the ribbon is popped into or out of its position (consult your Instruction quickly Booklet).

SI 1.03

S/A 17 (1 minute)

When we lived in Leith we could look out to the sea from our flat. Now, living in Louth, we have the coast still not far off, while the hills are near.

| | 1| . 2| 3| 4| 5| 6| 7| 8| 9| 1 0| 1 1| 1 2|

Top margin When a document runs to several pages, a good working method is to leave a uniform top margin of six lines of space (2.5 cm or 1 in) above the typing line, ie begin typing on the seventh line from the top of the sheet. On a first page however (or when the typewritten matter does not extend to a second and subsequent pages), it is customary to begin a few lines lower down. This is known as a dropped head. With A4 paper, a good working method for dropped heads is to leave nine lines of space and begin typing on the tenth line from the top of the sheet.

Setting side margins So far the margin positions have been given to you. You will now learn to decide them for yourself. In your future typewriting work, carefully consider (where you are not given specific instructions) the best margins to use. In particular, take into account the length of the task in relation to the size of paper being used.

Left- and right-hand margins may be equal, or the left margin may be wider than the right one. As a general rule it is bad practice for the right margin to be wider than the left one.

Equal side margins

Equal margins give a pleasing appearance and are particularly convenient if the work involves centred headings. (You always centre over the typing line, not over the width of the paper.) With equal margins, the centre point of the typing line and of the paper is the same. If you wish to leave equal margins of 2.5 cm (or 1 in) on A4 portrait or A5 landscape, you will set your margin stops as follows:

Elite type

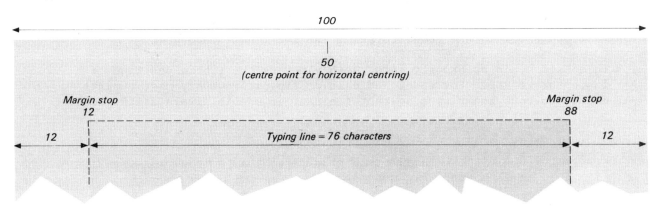

100

50
(centre point for horizontal centring)

Margin stop
12

Margin stop
88

12

Typing line = 76 characters

12

Pica type

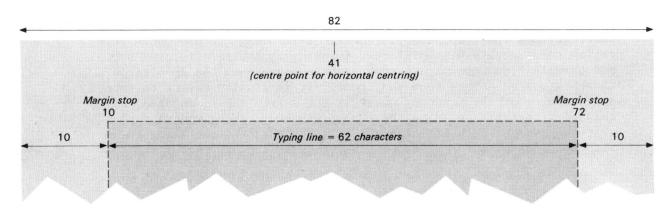

82

41
(centre point for horizontal centring)

Margin stop
10

Margin stop
72

10

Typing line = 62 characters

10

Checking work for errors (or proof reading, as this is often called) is an important part of a typist's work. In the office situation every piece of typewriting must be carefully checked for accuracy before being submitted as finished. Unmailable work is of no value.

Typewritten work should be read word for word, not just skimmed through—since our eyes have a way of passing over lines of typescript and seeing what we think should be there and not what we have actually typed. Some errors will not be obvious simply by reading the typescript. Particular attention should be paid to checking such points as correctness of dates, figures, addresses and proper nouns. Complete sentences are sometimes omitted by the typist and quite often words may be transposed or omitted. For all these reasons it is wise to check word for word with the original.

Each completed page of typescript should be checked before being removed from the typewriter—since corrections are so much easier to make when the paper is still in the machine.

Check the typing below for errors—it contains five mistakes.

Please look into the 2 letters of com-

plaint recieved from Hunt & Johnson

(account no 604537).   They allege

(wrongly I think) that we failed to

meet our delivery schedule; and that

our packing was inferior, resulting in

several breakages.   They are good cus-

tomers we do not wish to loose.

Manuscript

At times all typists have to type from a handwritten (manuscript) draft made by another person. Typing from manuscript is therefore an important part of a typist's skill.

1 Read through before typing Before starting to type, read through the whole manuscript, or at least far enough to be sure that the handwriting is clear to you. If the writing is difficult, study the way the writer forms letters in the words you can easily make out. A word that is at first difficult to read may be more obvious as you become familiar with the writing. Or it may be more legible when repeated later in the passage—perhaps more clearly shown, or in a context where the other words help suggest its meaning.

2 Spelling Typing from manuscript requires close attention to spelling. If you are in any doubt about the correct spelling of a word, you should consult a dictionary—which should always be to hand when you type. It is a good idea to keep a vocabularly notebook, as suggested in Unit 16 (5).

3 Drafting abbreviations To save time when writing a draft, many people use abbreviations—you probably do so yourself when taking notes. Examples are shd (should), wd (would) and recd (received). Many others occur—some in fairly common use but others simply an individual's choice.

Some writers of drafts always follow drafting abbreviations with a full stop to make clear that they are abbreviations. Others use a full stop only when the last letter of the abbreviation is not the last letter of the the word. Yet others use no stops at all (as in open punctuation). But be prepared for inconsistency in this matter. *The vital thing is that you identify the correct word for typing in full.*

Drafting abbreviations must always be clearly distinguished from generally used ones such as ie, eg, viz, etc, which should always be *typed in their abbreviated form*—just as they appear in print. (See page 47 for a list of drafting abbreviations.)

TECHNIQUE 9A   Checking for errors
Manuscript
Drafting abbreviations

46

5 On A4 paper, type the following advertisement in the centred style.

Target time: 20 minutes

OSCAR ROBINSON
(East Kirkby – Phone 702)

SHOP IN THE COUNTRY FOR COMFORT AND

BARGAINS

spaced caps and underscore

Freezers
Fridge/Freezers
Frozen Food
Groceries
Fancy Goods, Toys etc

* * * *

Large Car Park plus Children's Playground

OPEN: 1 pm to 8 pm Monday to Friday
9 am to 4 pm Saturday

6 Type the above advertisement in the blocked style.

Target time: 10 minutes

7 Prepare a layout sketch for the following notice. When you are satisfied you have divided the lines at natural points and given prominence to the key features, type it on A5 landscape paper. Use the centred style.

Target time: 15 minutes

Members of staff are invited to suggest advertisements for our products. Slogans are wanted like Sharp's Blades are Keen, with ideas for a suitable illustration. A prize of £50 goes to the best entry.

List A

accommodation	*accom.*	immediately	*immed.*	shall	*sh*
account	*a/c*	inconvenient/ence	*incon.*	should	*shd*
acknowledge	*ack.*	manufacturer	*mfr*	which	*wh*
advertisement	*advert.*	miscellaneous	*misc.*	would	*wd*
appointment	*appt.*	necessary	*necy*	with	*w*
approximately	*approx.*	opportunity	*opp.*	will	*wl*
believe	*bel.*	receipt	*rec.*	year	*yr*
business	*bus.*	receive	*rec.*	your	*yr*
catalogue	*cat.*	received	*recd*	dear	*dr*
committee	*cttee*	recommend	*recom.*		
company	*co.*	refer	*ref.*	days of the week (eg
companies	*cos.*	referred	*refd*	Thurs, Fri)
definitely	*def.*	responsible	*resp.*	months of the year
develop	*dev.*	secretary	*sec.*	(eg Jan, Feb)
exercise	*ex.*	separate	*sep.*	words in addresses
expense	*exp.*	signature	*sig.*	(eg Dr, Cres)
experience	*exp.*	sufficient	*suff.*	complimentary closes
government	*gov.*	temporary	*temp.*	(eg ffly)
guarantee	*gntee*	through	*thro'*	

List B

Note Other examining bodies and drafters in offices may use different and additional abbreviations to the ones listed above. However, these should present no problem when considered in context.

Amendments to text

You have already used most of the common correction signs and methods of amending text, listed below, but they are given again for consolidation and revision purposes.

a *Deletions without replacement text*—clearly crossed through to show the wording has been cancelled.
b *Deletions with replacement text*—the cancelled matter is clearly crossed through. The replacement text is written above the cancelled matter where possible; **or** written in the margin, with a caret sign at the point of insertion in the text (ie before or after the cancelled matter); **or** written in a balloon, with an arrow to the point of insertion (see below).
c *Balloons with arrows*—additional text is written in the 'balloon', and the arrow clearly shows where it is to be inserted.

Correction signs and their meaning

a ⌐ or // means start a new paragraph.

b ⌣⌒⌐ means reverse the order.

c ⸨⸩ or ⊇ means reverse the order vertically.

d ⟵⟶ means do not start a new paragraph.

e ⅄ (caret sign) means insert given matter here.

f ⊘ means retain the crossed through word(s) with dotted line below.

3 On A5 paper, type the following letter with a carbon copy, using today's date. Type a DL envelope and clip the papers together, as ready for signature.

Margins: elite—9 left, 64 right
pica—7 left, 54 right

Target time: 12 minutes

Ref BL/A/1063
Mrs S Andrews, 24 Wayside Walk, OXFORD OX3 4DB
Dr Madam
TRAVEL INSURANCE CLAIM
We acknowledge receipt of your claim forms dated (insert suitable date). However, we must return the Baggage + Personal Effects claim form to you as you have not given the purchase details which are required before we can proceed further with your claim. Likewise in this respect we will need a statement from the airline concerned confirming that yr diamond ring has not been recovered. Upon receipt of the above information we shall be pleased to give this matter our further attention.
Yrs ffly
NATIONWIDE HOLIDAY INSURANCE

4 On A4 paper, type the following letter with one carbon copy, using today's date. Type a DL envelope and assemble the papers as ready for signature.

Margins: elite—12 left, 90 right
pica—10 left, 75 right

Target time: 25 minutes

Mr D Jenkins, 87 Tennyson Rd, Golders Green, LONDON NW11 3BX
Dr Mr Jenkins   Mark this CONFIDENTIAL
We have been in touch in the past when I was working with Consulting Partners, Johnson + Ward.
I have now set up my own executive recruitment firm + wd like to ask yr help on an assignment I am currently handling for clients. The position is fully outlined by the enclosed specification. The client firm has been known to me personally for 3 yrs, during which time I have seen them grow from a one-man start into a well-managed + successful small company.
I think it possible that they will outgrow their US parent, such is the potential of the market they are in in Europe. While the job may not be of immediate interest to you, I shd be most grateful if you wd suggest any suitably qualified, capable young sales exec executives who wd like the exceptional opportunity of joining an expanding + exciting business.
I wd much appreciate any help you may be able to give us, + look forward to hearing from you as soon as possible.
Yrs sincerely
Ronald Clark

untapped
personal

My new flat is only 5 km from my job - which saves me a
tiring bus/train journey of 25 km each way. For my bedroom
I need a carpet 4 m x 3 m and a pair of curtains, each
2½ m x 2 m. A small side window requires a single curtain
95 cm x 86 cm. On my coffee table I want a glass top
measuring 951 mm x 748 mm.

Technique Section 9 (pages 46 and 47)

On a sheet of A4 paper, type the two following passages, taking one carbon copy.
Begin typing on the tenth line down from the top of the page. Use blocked
paragraphs. Note the method (illustrated in the last line of **a**) of clarifying a badly
written word.)

Margins: elite—18 left, 85 right
pica—15 left, 70 right

Type **a** in double spacing.

a

Many people know that their handwriting is far from clear.
Sometimes they cannot even read it themselves, so they shd
not be surprised when others can't read it ! Some of these
people take pains to write slowly ~~and distinctly~~ when it is
important that there should be no mistake or misunderstanding.
There is, however, one simple aid to clarity which many people
~~often~~ ignore. Use a |pencil|or|pen|with a sharp point : never
pencil   use a blunt/ or a ball-point pen w a smudgy tip.   (SMUDGY)

Use the carriage return twice before starting **b**. Type **b** in single spacing (double
between paragraphs). Leave one line of space below Dear Sir and above Yours
faithfully; no comma after each of these.

b

Dr Sir
In view of the damage from fallen trees wh we saw around us
last winter, I have taken advice on the condition of the trees on
my property. [There is a large beech tree which is ~~considered~~
unsafe in the severe gales which often occur in this region.]
I am especially concerned about this tree since it is close to
both my neighbour's house and my own.
I therefore request the consent of my Local Authority to
have this tree felled.
Because of my anxiety, I hope to rec. an early reply.
Yrs ffly

SI 1.10

Take care to sit well when you type. Keep both your feet on
the floor, one slightly in front of the other. See that you
place your copy on your right.

| 1| 2| 3| 4| 5| 6| 7| 8| 9| 10| 11| 12|

Next morning, viewing the green fields against an azure sky, we were quite decided that this was the day to join in a climbing expedition.

1 *Technique Section 14F (page 76)*

When you have checked the calculations, type the menu on A4 paper, centring each line horizontally and the whole vertically. If your typewriter has an asterisk key (*), type three spaced asterisks between courses. Otherwise use three spaced hyphens.

2 *a* On another sheet of A4 paper, type the same menu again—but this time in the blocked style of layout. Between courses, extend unspaced asterisks or hyphens as far as the longest item in the course above. This helps to balance up the material in the blocked style. (2 ringed errors to correct.)

$$\text{T H E} \quad \text{C A S T L E} \quad \text{H O T E L}$$

CHICHESTER, SUSSEX

Luncheon Menu

Tomato Soup
~~and~~
Grapefruit

* * * * * * * * * *

Fried Fillet of Place - Sauce Tartare
Roast Chicken, Stuffing and Bread Sauce

French Fried Potatoes
Roast and Creamed Potatos
Fresh Garden Peas
Buttered Carrots

* *

Peach Melba
Fruit Tart
or
Cheese and Biscuits

* * * * * * * * * * * * * * * *

Coffee

b Compare your two typed examples of the menu. Which method of display do you prefer? Do you think the extra time spent in centring was worth while?

SI 1.39

Many people do not use the public libraries or know the full range of services which they provide. Lending libraries not only offer the books on their shelves, but if asked will get others for home reading. Most reference sections have books on a broad range of questions.

| 1| 2| 3| 4| 5| 6| 7| 8| 9| 1 0| 1 1| 1 2|

It is recognized that the ability to check work quickly is a vital part of typewriting skill. Spelling and exact alignment are just 2 points to watch for.

1   On a sheet of A4 paper, type the two following passages, taking one carbon copy. Begin typing on the tenth line down from the top of the page. Use blocked paragraphs.

Margins: elite—18 left, 85 right
            pica—15 left, 70 right

Type **a** in double spacing.

a

Everyone's
~~Each of our~~ homes has a postcode + we are often asked to use it in our correspondence. Postcodes were introduced ~~in Britain~~ Ⓥ after a team of 20 people spent 2 yrs preparing them. The idea behind postcodes is to cut to a minimum the man-handling of ~~mail~~ letters - although the postman who delivers our letters wd be hard to replace! The postcode shd always be the last item on an envelope and, because of the electronic sorting equipment, it shd <u>not be punctuated in any way</u>. There shd be / spaces between the 2 parts of the postcode.

b

Use the carriage return twice before starting **b**. Type **b** in single spacing (double between paragraphs). Leave one line of space below Dear Sir and above Yours faithfully; no comma after each of these.

Dr Sir

I have pleasure in enclosing my cheque for £15 as my subscription to the Residents Society for the coming yr. As I am moving from the district I must give notice that this will be my last yr of membership. I shd like to express my appreciation of the assistance and friendship that I have recd from the Society.
Yrs ffly

SI 1.12

I wrote to you before Christmas to ask if you could offer me a job as a clerk in your office. You said that I should try in June. This I am now doing.

| 1 | 2 | 3 | 4 | 5 | 6 | 7 | 8 | 9 | 10 | 11 | 12 |

When a piece of display is too large to fit well on A5 paper, A4 should be used. There may be other occasions when A4 would be preferred—for instance if plenty of white space round the display was wanted.

1 **Character spaces across A4 paper (portrait)** You will see from the paper diagram on page 54 that A4 paper measures 210 mm × 297 mm (approx $8\frac{1}{4}$ in × $11\frac{3}{4}$ in). Therefore, as with A5 landscape, you can type 100 characters (elite) or 82 characters (pica) across the page. Centre point of A4 paper (for horizontal centring) is therefore 50 or 41.

2 **Lines of space down A4 paper** Since A4 paper measures 297 mm (approx $11\frac{3}{4}$ in) down the page, there are 70 lines with both elite and pica type.

3 **Horizontal and vertical centring on A4 paper** Knowing these figures, you can centre on A4 paper, applying the methods you have used already for A5 paper.

Because of its length, the following menu would look best typed on A4 paper. For effective display, the number of lines of space between the different parts varies.

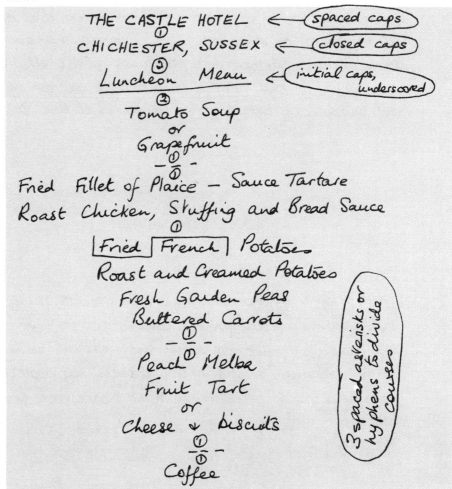

a The total number of lines the menu will occupy is 32.
b 70 − 32 = 38.
c 38 ÷ 2 = 19.
d Therefore you will centre the first line on the twentieth line down from the top of the paper.
e Take care to use the carriage return the correct number of times between the lines of the menu, in order to leave the number of lines of space you allowed for in the calculation.

On a sheet of A4 paper, type the two following passages. Begin typing on the tenth line down from the top of the page.

Margins: elite—18 left, 85 right
pica—15 left, 70 right

Type **1** in double spacing. (4 ringed errors to correct.)

1

Target time: 15 minutes

OPEN PUNCTUATION ON ENVELOPES   *leave 2 lines of space here*

Open punctuation on envelopes means the omission of ~~virtually~~ all ✓ punctuation marks. There is no comma at the end of each line or full-stop at the end of the address, as was the case with the tradition(all) method. Abbreviations are typed with open punctuation (as was explained ~~to you~~ in Technique Section 4). When it/is coupled with the blocked style of layout, open punctuation on envelopes is a good example of simplifying and speeding up the work of the typist. The simplicity of the style also assists clarity of understanding. Copy the following name and address in the open-punctuated, blocked style, exactly as shown. Note that in every line there is <u>one</u> space between the different parts.

Mr T S Waters CBE BSc
24 Park Avenue
CROYDON
CR6 2PQ

 *single spacing*

With open punctuation on envelopes, just a few necessary pu(n)t(u)ation marks remain, like the apostrophe in Penny's Pantry and a hyphen (or solidu(s)) divi(s)ing 2 street numbers, like 28-34 Union Street.

Use the carriage return twice before starting **2**. Type **2** in single spacing, but leave one line of space below Dear Sir and above Yours faithfully.

2

Target time: 3 minutes

Dr Sir

Thank you for yr letter of 15 April. In answer to yr query —
my interest in the position offered is such that I wd
gladly move to York or Bristol if the need arose.
I am sorry I did not make this clear on my Application
Form.

Yrs ffly

A zither is a musical instrument with metal strings fixed over a flat wooden frame which rests on a table or just on the player's knees. It should not be confused with the sitar, an Indian instrument quite like a long-necked guitar.

1 *Technique Section 14E (page 74)*

On A5 portrait paper, type the piece of display headed *Darwin Travel*, centring each line horizontally and the whole vertically.

2 On another sheet of A5 portrait paper, type the following notice. Centre each line horizontally.

MORGAN, JONES & EVANS LTD

①

STAFF SOCIAL CLUB

②

Committee Officers

①

Chairman: Stanley P Edwards
Vice-Chairman: William Brown
Secretary: Geoffrey J Williams
Treasurer: Catherine Gill } single spacing

②

AIMS and OBJECTS

①

To promote friendship and fellowship
among members of the staff
through social activities of all kinds

3 On A5 portrait paper, type the above notice again. This time use the blocked style of layout.

SI 1.37

There are many good reasons why holidays abroad are popular. One of them is simply that it is refreshing to live for even a short time in a strange country and learn its customs. As knowledge of the language is so useful, it is worth learning some common words and phrases.

| 1| 2| 3| 4| 5| 6| 7| 8| 9| 10| 11| 12|

1   The name and address should always be typed parallel to the longer side of the envelope.

2   Each part of the address should be typed on a separate line.

3   The town should be typed in closed capitals.

4   Except in the case of a few large cities (Manchester, Birmingham, Edinburgh, etc—a full list is given in the *Post Office Guide*) the county should be typed as well.

5   The postcode should always be typed last. Because of the electronic sorting equipment, the postcode should not be punctuated or underscored. There should be one space between its two parts. If the postcode is typed on the same line as the town or county, leave two spaces in front of it.

6   If, for special attention, the letter is to be marked Personal, Urgent, Confidential, etc, this should be typed above the name (where it will be immediately visible), and separated from it by at least one line of space. Such information can be typed in closed capitals, or with initial capitals and underscored.

7   The first line of the name and address should be typed about half way down the envelope, so that the address appears in the lower half. The name and address should be approximately centred horizontally. These positions on the envelope should be estimated, not measured in any way—this will be easy with practice.

8   The quickest way to type envelopes is to use the blocked method and open punctuation, so that the left-hand margin can be set at the point where each line will begin. Use single or 1½ line spacing—the latter makes the address more legible. Use double spacing if the address is very short or when using large envelopes.

The following examples illustrate some of the above points.

```
PERSONAL

Mrs S Cole
42 Court Road
MANCHESTER
M16 6AL
```

```
Mr T L Bond
25 Longton Road
EXETER
Devon
EX5 2PQ
```

```
D Ross Esq
8 Lee Rise
WATFORD
Herts   WD3 4AP
```

```
Urgent

Miss C Day
26 West Road
LONDON   SW9 5ET
```

When to use A5 landscape or A5 portrait

The 'shape' of a piece of display should always be considered when deciding how to use the paper. If the lines are few but fairly wide, A5 landscape is more suitable. When the display is fairly long but narrow, the portrait style would be a better choice.

1 **Character spaces across A5 portrait** A5 portrait measures 148 mm × 210 mm (approx 5⅞ in × 8¼ in). Therefore you can type 70 (elite) or 58 (pica) cnaracters across the page. Centre point of A5 portrait (for horizontal centring) is 35 (elite). 29 (pica).

2 **Lines of space down A5 portrait** Since A5 portrait measures 210 mm (approx 8¼ in) down the page, there are 50 lines with both elite and pica type.

3 **Horizontal and vertical centring on A5 portrait** Knowing the above figures, you can centre on A5 portrait, applying the methods you have used for A5 landscape.

Because it is long but narrow, the notice below would look well typed on A5 portrait paper.

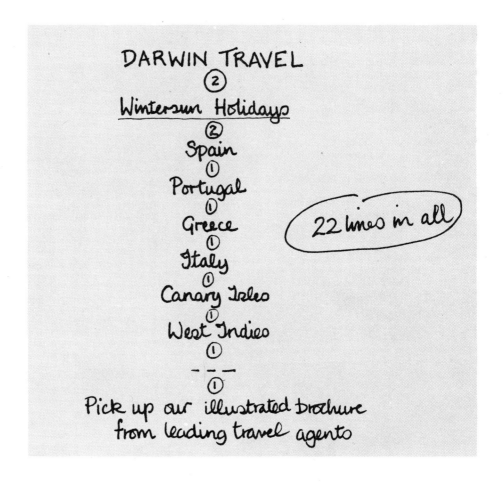

a The total number of lines the display will occupy is 22.
b 50 − 22 = 28.
c 28 ÷ 2 = 14.
d Therefore the first line of the notice will be typed on the fifteenth line down from the top of a sheet of A5 portrait paper (to leave 14 lines clear above and below the typing).

Courtesy titles

1   Ms is used for married or unmarried women. It should be used if the marital status is unknown or if the person concerned prefers this form of address.

```
Miss L Barker
Mrs B Adams
Ms C Watson
```

2   Mr or Esq—one or the other should be used when addressing a man. It is incorrect to use both.

```
Mr L J Henderson
T Watts Esq
```

The Rev or Rev (for a clergyman) or Dr (for a doctor) replace Mr or Esq.

```
The Rev C Baker
Dr A T Little
```

3   Messrs is used when addressing a partnership. However, Messrs is often omitted if there are three or more names. (Note that a comma is necessary in this example to make it clear that there are three names.)

```
Messrs Watson & James

Thomas, Lock & Brown
```

4   No courtesy title is used:

a   when a title is included in a name;

```
Dame Elizabeth Winters DBE
Sir James Winterbottom KCB
```

b   when the name of a firm is impersonal or begins with 'the' etc;

```
Maythorpe Engineering
The Fenton Electrical Co
```

c   before the name of a limited company;

```
Modown Electrical Co Ltd
```

d   with some 'professional' names.

```
Helen Kay Fashions
Janet Jay, Editor
```

Decorations, honours and qualifications should be typed in their correct order. As a general rule, they are listed in order of importance, as follows:

1   Decorations and honours
    (Military and civil):   VC (Victoria Cross)
                                   MC (Military Cross)
                                   CBE (Commander of the British
                                   Empire) etc.

```
Mr T Smithson VC
```

2   Educational qualifications: MA (Master of Arts)
                                   BSc (Bachelor of Science) etc.

```
Mrs E Thomas CBE MA
```

3   Professional titles: FRCS (Fellow of the Royal College
                                   of Surgeons)
                                   FRSA (Fellow of the Royal Society
                                   of Arts) etc.

```
Mr B Maitland MC BSc FRSA
```

4   Member of Parliament: MP

```
Mrs A Swan CBE MP
```

Note   Educational and professional qualifications are usually omitted except in some formal correspondence.

Window envelopes

Window envelopes have cut from the front a panel that is covered with transparent paper, through which the inside address on the enclosed letter appears. The typist is therefore saved the time of typing an address on the envelope.

The position for typing the name and address on the headed paper used with window envelopes is indicated by a ruled box, or by dots or short right angles. Correct and careful folding is essential when window envelopes are being used, to ensure that the name and address are fully visible through the 'window'. Some printed stationery has one or two fold marks on the left-hand edge of the paper to aid the typist.

The signs of the zodiac are named after constellations. Examples are Libra and Aquarius. In what is called judicial astrology, their movements are supposed to influence luck and fortune.

1 *Technique Section 14D (page 72)*

Using a sheet of A5 landscape paper for each, type the two notices, centring them horizontally and vertically.

2 Prepare a layout sketch for the following. When you are satisfied that you have divided the lines at natural points and given prominence to the key features, type it on A5 landscape. Centre each line horizontally and the whole vertically.

Come to our Bargains Galore Jumble Sale on Saturday 4 May 19—— at 3pm. All proceeds in aid of Help the Aged Fund. Admission 25p.

3 On A5 landscape paper, type the following notice in the blocked style, centring it vertically on the page. Set the left-hand margin stop at the point you would begin centring the longest line. Decide yourself on the space to leave between lines.

A GARDEN FETE — (spaced caps)
will be held at
Riverview Gardens, Outwood
on
Saturday 24 June at 3.30pm
in aid of
THE PARISH CHURCH RESTORATION FUND
Entrance 95p
Raffle, Sideshows, Bring-and-Buy Stall

4 Using A6 landscape (see pages 54 and 114 for size and scales) prepare and type suitable *tickets* relating to the notices typed in 2 and 3 above: then a ticket for the concert given on page 72.

SI 1.34

Most firms choose with great care the person whose job it is to answer the telephone. They realise that he or she should have a pleasant speaking voice and always be most polite and helpful in manner. No one should be left waiting at the end of a line without explanation.

| | 1| | 2| | 3| | 4| | 5| | 6| | 7| | 8| | 9| | 1 0| | 1 1| | 1 2|

This boy is judged too lazy to do the work required in the sixth form. He must either be kept back a year or leave school.

1 *Technique Section 10A (page 51)*

Copy the four examples illustrated on DL envelopes (110 mm × 222 mm: approx $4\frac{1}{4}$ in × $8\frac{5}{8}$ in). If envelopes cannot be obtained for practice purposes, use a sheet of A4 paper folded into three (use all the 'faces'). Do not use single slips of DL size paper; they are difficult to use and do not give the correct 'feel'.
Use the blocked style with open punctuation. Use single spacing. It will help if you put a light pencil × where you will begin typing—until with practice you know where to start.

2 *Technique Section 10B (page 52)*

On the same sheet of paper as you used for the drill above, copy the examples of forms and addresses, etc, which are typed down the right-hand side of page 52 (one per line in double spacing).
Carefully note and follow the spacing and punctuation in each example. Set your left-hand margin position at elite 25, pica 20. Move the right-hand stop to the extreme right position.

3 Type envelopes in the blocked style, with open punctuation (as you did in **1** above) for the following:

a Mrs L Holt, 24 Main Street, Eastbourne, Sussex, BN21 1EH
b T Lane Esq, 13 Devonshire Place, Coventry, CV4 6MN
     The enclosed letter is confidential.
c Miss P Goodwin, 18 Lakeside Road, Ipswich, IP3 2XN
d Sir John Small KBE, 27 Oak Tree Avenue, Romford, Essex, RM2 4LX
     Show that the letter is personal.
e Messrs Faith & Longwood, 40–42 Park Road, Southampton, SO2 6JB
f Mr J Rogers, 13 Riverview Road, Dublin, Eire.

4 Type envelopes for the following. This time use $1\frac{1}{2}$ line spacing:

a Rev J Stanton, Rectory Close, Wakefield, Yorkshire, WF6 5TS

b Mrs B Robinson, 22 Tennyson Road, London SW19 5PQ

c Mr F White, Regent Fashions Ltd, 14/16 Malt Lane, Wolverhampton, WV6 2PL

d James, Webb & Mason, 20 Clarendon Road, Padstow, Cornwall, PL3 2TS

e Ms P Watson, 8 The Meadows, Gloucester, GL2 3BA

f Dr P Connolly, 79 Wembley Drive, Wembley, Middx, HA3 5SQ

SI 1.13

S/A 20 (1 minute)

The school to be built next year will take boys and girls of junior school age. There will still be a lack of places for students in senior age groups.

| 1| 2| 3| 4| 5| 6| 7| 8| 9| 10| 11| 12|

Sometimes you will need to prepare for yourself a layout of a piece of display. This is a sketch showing the display, line by line, indicating the style to be used for each line (spaced capitals, closed capitals, underscored, etc) and the number of spaces to be left between lines.

1 For instance, you could be asked to set out in display form the following:

> Come to Green Mountain Farm, York, for your holiday. Delightful setting and sports facilities. Write to the proprietor, Mr A Day, for full details

A suggested layout for A5 landscape follows. The figures in circles show the number of lines of space to leave (ten lines in all).

> COME TO ← spaced caps
> ①
> GREEN MOUNTAIN FARM, YORK
> ①
> for your holiday
> ②
> DELIGHTFUL SETTING AND SPORTS FACILITIES
> ①
> Write to the proprietor, Mr A Day, for full details

2 Another A5 landscape example follows:

> A Variety Concert in aid of the Cancer Research Foundation will be held on Friday 29 September 19__ at 8pm in The Town Hall, Oldminster, Admission £1·50

Here is a suggested layout:

> A VARIETY CONCERT ← spaced caps
> ①
> in aid of
> ①
> THE CANCER RESEARCH FOUNDATION
> ①
> will be held on
> ①
> Friday 29 September 19__
> ①
> at 8pm in
> The Town Hall, Oldminster
> ①
> Admission £1·50

Features of good layout

Carefully note how, in both examples, the lines have been divided at natural points. Key features have been given prominence—for clarity and impact.

From now on you will use A5 paper as well as A4. The **A sizes of paper** now in general use (called IPS—for International Paper Sizes) are based on a rectangle that keeps the same proportions each time it is halved. The original size is A0. A1 is half the size of A0; A2 is half the size of A1, and so on. Thus the higher the figure that follows the A, the smaller is the paper. The diagram below will make this clear.

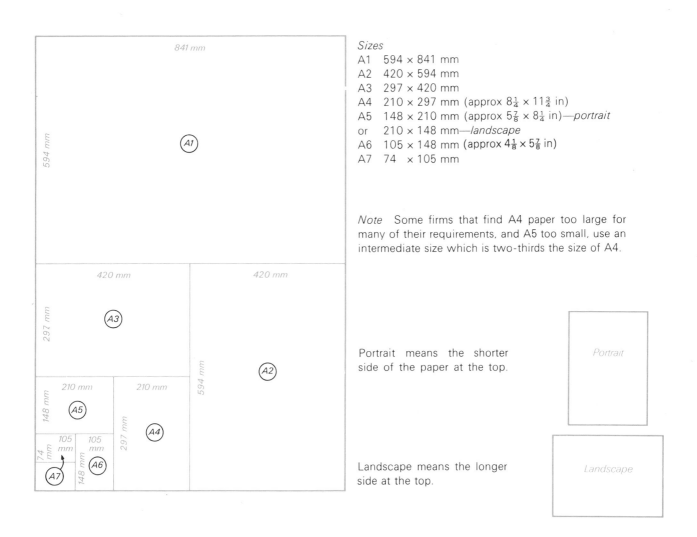

Sizes
A1   594 × 841 mm
A2   420 × 594 mm
A3   297 × 420 mm
A4   210 × 297 mm (approx $8\frac{1}{4}$ × $11\frac{3}{4}$ in)
A5   148 × 210 mm (approx $5\frac{7}{8}$ × $8\frac{1}{4}$ in)—*portrait*
or   210 × 148 mm—*landscape*
A6   105 × 148 mm (approx $4\frac{1}{8}$ × $5\frac{7}{8}$ in)
A7   74   × 105 mm

Note   Some firms that find A4 paper too large for many of their requirements, and A5 too small, use an intermediate size which is two-thirds the size of A4.

Portrait means the shorter side of the paper at the top.

Landscape means the longer side at the top.

The relationship between A4 and A5 paper

1   Place a sheet of A4 paper on your desk with the shorter side at the top (portrait).

2   Fold it exactly in half from bottom to top, and make a sharp crease along the middle. The paper on either side of the crease will represent an A5 sheet of paper. Thus A5 is exactly half the size of A4.

3   Check the measurements of both A4 and A5 with a ruler and the figures given on the diagram above.

4   Cut, or carefully tear with the aid of a ruler, your sheet of A4 paper along the crease. Keep these two sheets of A5 paper for later use.

In June the azaleas make a splash of exquisite colour behind the fountain, ranging through every shade of pink, red and yellow.

1 *Technique Section 14C (page 70)*

Centre the task illustrated, vertically and horizontally.

2 On another sheet of A5 landscape, centre the following notice both horizontally and vertically. Leave one line of space after each line of type.

Longdon Motors Limited ← (closed caps)
Personal Assistant
required for
Marketing Director
Interested secretaries in all Departments
are invited to contact the
Personnel Officer

3 On A5 landscape paper, type the notice below in blocked style. Centre it vertically. Set your left-hand margin stop at the point you would start centring the longest line. The ringed figures show the number of lines of space to leave between the different parts. (2 ringed errors to correct.)

O L D T O W N   T E N N I S   C L U B
②

ANNUAL DINNER
①
at the White Swan Restaraunt
Oldtown
①
on
①
Friday 10 February 19--
①
1930 hrs for 2000 hrs
①
Tickets £4.50p single

SI 1.35

One of the merits of learning to type is that your skill can be put to good personal use. Typed letters are easy to read and in business matters tend to get better attention. Often it is handy to keep a carbon copy of what was said. One can readily think of further uses.

| 1| 2| 3| 4| 5| 6| 7| 8| 9| 10| 11| 12|

Everyone is familiar, to some degree, with the layout and various styles of business letters. Many firms now use the fully-blocked style (every line beginning at the left-hand margin) and open punctuation—since it is the easiest and quickest form to type.

Carefully study the following example of part of a fully-blocked letter with open punctuation and note the descriptions of the various parts. (A complete letter should always include the date. This is introduced in Technique Section 12B on page 57.)

Note   The ringed figures between the parts of the letter show the number of lines of space left. (See also box at foot of page 57.)

Inside name and address   This records the name and address of the person to whom the letter is being sent (the addressee). It ensures that each letter is inserted in its correct envelope and enables the carbon copy to be filed correctly.

It is always typed in single spacing—in the same way as on the envelope. Each part begins on a new line (although the postcode need not be) and the town should be typed in capital letters.

Salutation   This is the greeting that opens a letter. It will usually appear as Dear Sir, Dear Sirs, Dear Madam, Dear Mr Jones, Dear Mrs Turner, etc.

```
Mr T Watkins
64 Old Park Road
CATERHAM
Surrey  CR3 6LH
       ②
Dear Sir
       ①
Thank you for your letter informing us that you wish to
sell your house.
       ①
Property in the Old Park district is not easy to sell
because of the proposed new motorway.  However, if the
price is right, a buyer can usually be found as there
is a shortage of houses for sale in the Caterham area.
       ①
We propose sending our Mr Forbes round to inspect the
property and would suggest next Saturday morning at
11 am.
       ①
Yours faithfully
```

Complimentary close   This is typed below the body of the letter. The most common forms are Yours faithfully, Yours truly, Yours sincerely—the first word only beginning with a capital letter.

Body of the letter   This is the subject matter of the letter and it is divided into paragraphs.

TECHNIQUE 12A A5 letters   Inside name and address   **55**
Salutation
Body of letter
Complimentary close

When typing any piece of display, you will want to position it well vertically on the paper. Many people agree that equal space above and below the typescript looks best. You will now learn how to centre a piece of display vertically on the page.

1 Calculating lines of space down a page With both pica and elite pitch there are *six* lines of typing in single spacing to each 2.5 cm (or 1 in). Test this for yourself by typing your name six times in single spacing on a spare piece of paper: use a new line each time. Remove the paper and measure the six lines of typing vertically, from top to bottom.

A5 landscape measures 210 mm × 148 mm (approx $8\frac{1}{4}$ in × $5\frac{7}{8}$ in). Thus there are 35 lines down the page.

2 Example for vertical display on A5 landscape The following display and the instructions below will clarify the procedure of vertical centring. One line of space is left between the lines of type in this example.

W O O D S T O C K   L I B E R A L   A S S O C I A T I O N

We Invite You and Your Friends to

A SHERRY PARTY

on

Wednesday 6 October

1830 hrs

at

Linden, Green Park Road, Woodstock

Entrance £1.50 (including raffle)

Method for vertical display on A5 landscape

1 Count the total number of lines the display will occupy, from start to finish, counting both lines of type and lines of space between the typing. (In the above case it is 17.)

2 Subtract this figure from 35—the number of lines down the page. (35 − 17 = 18.)

3 Divide the result by two, to find out how many lines will appear equally above and below the typing. If this answer results in a fraction, ignore it. (18 ÷ 2 = 9. Thus there will be nine lines of space above the typing and nine lines of space below it.)

4 Set the line-space selector at 1 and insert a sheet of A5 landscape in your typewriter.

5 Move the margin stops out of the way—to the extreme right and left positions.

6 With the right-hand cylinder knob, adjust the paper so that its top edge is flush with the alignment scale.

7 From the top edge of the paper, use the carriage return once more than the answer arrived at in 3 above; this is because you will begin typing on this line. (In the example, you will use the carriage return ten times—to leave nine lines above the typing.)

8 Clear any existing tab stops and then set a tab stop at the centre point of the paper.

9 Now proceed to type each line of the display, centring it horizontally in the style shown. Return the carriage twice after each line, in order to leave the one line of space planned.

In the zoo, very wild animals like tigers and jackals are
kept in cages. Harmless animals, like oxen, have quite open
fields to roam in.

1 *Technique Section 11 (page 54)*

As instructed, fold a sheet of A4 paper to make two sheets of A5 size.

2 *Technique Section 12A (page 55)*

Copy the part-letter on plain A5 paper (portrait). Begin typing on the tenth
line down from the top of the page.

Margins: elite—9 left, 64 right
          pica—7 left, 54 right

3   Using plain A5 paper, type the two following letters in the same style as
task **2**. Take a carbon copy of the second one. Begin typing in the same place and
use the same margins as in task **2**. (Letters should contain a date: you will learn
how and where to type the date in the next Technique Section. For the present,
omit the date.)

a   Mrs S Brown
      47 Lake View Road
      HUDDERSFIELD
      HD4 6PU

      Dear Madam

      We thank you for your letter of yesterday's date and
      confirm that we are able to cater for small birthday
      parties. //We will send full details of our programmes
      and tariffs at the end of next week - as soon as we
      receive new copies from the printers.

      Yours truly

b   Miss W Davis, Homelea, 27 Aston Rd, MAIDSTONE,
      Dear Miss Davis   Kent ME5 2AL
                  Thank you for yr letter enclosing a cheque in
      additional, full settlement payment of the curtain fabric & accessories
      that you ordered by telephone. [As requested, the
      goods have been sent to yr curtain-maker at
      the chatham address you supplied.
      Yrs sincerely

SI 1.20

It is easy to recognize a skilled typist. Not only does she
type fast but she also does things the right way. Watch how
she sits and holds her wrists.

| 1| 2| 3| 4| 5| 6| 7| 8| 9| 10| 11| 12|

Even at the zebra crossing extreme care should be taken in crossing this wide road, as cars appear so quickly just from nowhere.

1 *Technique Section 14B* (*page 68*)

Type the two displayed pieces.

2 On another sheet of A5 landscape, centre the following multi-line display. Use the carriage return 15 times from the top of the page before typing the first line. Leave one line of space between lines of type.

F A N T A S T I C   S P R I N G   S A L E

of

COATS AND DRESSES

For Town and Country

centre
each
line

3 On another sheet of A5 landscape paper, type the display below in blocked style. Begin typing on the twelfth line from the top of the paper. The ringed figures show the number of lines of space to leave between the different parts. Centre the longest line and set the left-hand margin where this line begins. Start all the lines at this point.

N E W T O W N   C O L L E G E
①
offers
①
EVENING CLASSES
①
in
①
Shorthand
Typewriting
English
Accounts
Office Practice

SI 1.28

S/A 27 (2 minutes)

That we should read a good newspaper has been impressed upon us all since our youth. But it really is sound advice. Not only do we need to keep abreast of events in our own country and in the world, but what the news means is made clearer in leading articles and features.

| 1| 2| 3| 4| 5| 6| 7| 8| 9| 10| 11| 12|

Reference(s) These are used to trace and file correspondence. The letterhead may have a printed place for them. Otherwise they are typed as in this example. The reference frequently consists of the capital letter initials of the person who dictated the letter, followed by the initials of the typist (the latter sometimes in small letters). The reference may also indicate the department of the firm and/or a file number. The different parts of the reference may be divided by a solidus or a full stop—but there should be no full stop at the end. A letter in reply to one containing a reference should quote this reference first—as in the example.

Letterhead Most firms use paper with their name, address and other information printed at the top. (Where possible, align your left margin to the letterhead.)
If you practise typing business letters on paper without a letterhead, leave nine lines of space at the top of A5 portrait and twelve lines at the top of A4.

Sussex House
24 Park Road
London WC2D 4AP

Swan Electrical Limited

Telephone: 01–242 8736
Telex: 708642

SWAN

②

```
Your ref TLW.PT
Our ref  GKR.mp
```

②

```
20 October 19--
```

②

```
Messrs Webb & Wainwright
20/22 Hill View Road
ILFORD
Essex  IG2 4BA
```

②

```
Dear Sirs
```

①

```
Thank you for your letter of 18 October requesting 5
instruction leaflets for our Radio, Serial No MPG 112.
In fact these were despatched 3 days ago, following
your telephone call.  We trust they have now reached
you.
```

①

```
Yours faithfully
```

Date The recommended order is day, month, year—typed as shown here. When you type letters, always use the date of typing, unless you have instructions to the contrary.

Spacing above salutation There is no hard and fast rule here. However, if you always use the spacing shown in these letters, it will help to speed up your typing of letters.

Note Open punctuation in letters means omitting virtually all punctuation except in the body of the letter (and postscript). There the punctuation is full—except where the open-punctuated method of typing abbreviations is used (*see* page 31). Open punctuation goes well with a blocked style of layout, as used in the letters in this book.

1 **Horizontal centring of multi-lines on A5 land-scape** If you need to centre a heading or notice that consists of several lines, merely centre each line, one by one, as you have done already. It will help if you set a tab stop at the centre point of the paper.

2 **Heading devices** To produce effective and pleasing work, you will want to give prominence to certain aspects in a heading—by use of the various heading devices shown below.

Note how, in the following example, the various key items stand out.

```
Z E N I T H   R E N T A L   C O M P A N Y        spaced capitals
                    ①
                   for                           small letters
                    ①
          LOW-COST COLOUR TV                     closed capitals
                    ①
         From Only £15.50 Down                   initial capitals,
                                                 underscored
```

The first line is in spaced capitals:

a One space between letters in the words.
b Three spaces between words.
c There are 41 characters in all in this line. You will therefore backspace 20 times from the centre point of the paper, before beginning to type (taking the letters/ spaces two at a time, ignoring the odd letter left over).

3 **Apply heading devices** Type the above example on a sheet of A5 landscape paper, observing the following points:

a Set the line-space selector at position 1.
b Move margin stops out of the way—to the extreme right and left positions.

c Adjust the paper so that its top edge is flush with the top of the alignment scale.
d Use the carriage return 15 times.
e Set a tab stop at the centre point of the page.

Centre and copy line by line, leaving one line of space between lines of type (by using the carriage return twice between each line). If you have carried out the instructions carefully and correctly, you will see that your typing is pleasingly centred on the paper.

4 **Varying the vertical space** Sometimes, for effect, you will want to vary the number of lines of space between lines of type. The following example illustrates this.

```
      T H E   C A S T L E   H O T E L
                    ①
          CHICHESTER, SUSSEX
                    ②

        A Famous Historic Inn
                    ①
      WRITE FOR OUR COMPREHENSIVE TARIFF
```

Centre and copy this example on a sheet of A5 land-scape. Proceed as you did in the previous example, but use the carriage return 14 times from the top of the page before starting to type.
Take care to leave the indicated space between lines.

All even numbers can be divided by 2 - 24, 518, 38, 198.
All numbers ending in 5 or 0 can be divided evenly by 5 -
10, 215, 45, 385.

1 *Technique Section 12B (page 57)*

Type the letter in the Technique Section on an A5 printed letterhead. Take care to leave the indicated number of lines of space between the different parts of the letter: these are ringed on the copy.

Margins: elite—9 left, 64 right
         pica—7 left, 54 right

2 Type the two following letters on A5 letterheads, using the same style and margins as in the last task. Take a carbon copy of **b**. (Do not forget to insert the date.)

a

Our ref CJB.pt.3185

Mrs RG Rowlands, 2 Firs Lane, Nottingham, NG2 4AS
Dear Mrs Rowlands
We were pleased to receive your letter of yesterday's date, telling us of yr friends who wd like to be on our regular mailing list. [You will be interested to learn that, from next July, we shall be issuing our full catalogue quarterly instead of half yearly.
Yrs sincerely

b

Our ref JPW.ed
T Balfour Esq, 37 Cromwell Road, LUTON, Beds, LU5 2TS
Dr Sir
Thank you for yr letter informing us of yr change of address. I am afraid we have no record of yr having notified us of the change earlier this year.//If you will send us yr Passbook, we will credit yr accrued interest.

Yrs ffly

SI 1.08

S/A 22 (2 minutes)

The telephone has a big place in our lives, both at work and in the home. More and more use is made of it both for local and long-distance calls. The great thing is to be clear and brief, so that you keep down the cost and do not waste time.

   1   2   3   4   5   6   7   8   9   10   11   12

Exciting ships of every size were to be seen in the docks and in the estuary just beyond - from quaint old merchant vessels to modern liners.

1 *Technique Section 14A (page 66)*

Following the instructions given, centre the line *Report on New Office Filing System* on A5 landscape paper.

2 Continuing on the same sheet of A5 paper, centre the following lines. Leave one line of space between lines of type (by using the carriage return twice in single spacing).

Summer Catalogue of Sportswear

Sale of Raincoats and Showerproofs

Houses for Sale and to Let

Use shift lock   COSMETIC AND TOILET PRODUCTS

MOUNTSIDE ART GALLERY

If you have followed the instructions correctly, each of these lines should be well centred on the page. In addition, each one should be centred with all the others.

3 The following passage is a single piece of display. On another sheet of A5 landscape, type the display in the **blocked style**. Begin typing on the twelfth line from the top of the page. Centre the longest line (*Summer Catalogue of Sportswear*). Set the left-hand margin stop at the beginning of this line and begin all lines at this point. Set the line space selector at 2 (to leave one line of space between lines).

SUMMER CATALOGUE OF SPORTSWEAR

See Our Latest Fashions in

Ladies' Tennis Dresses

Men's Golfing Windcheaters

Ladies' Co-ordinates

Men's Co-ordinates

Children's Sportswear

SI 1.37

More and more people are using bicycles to get themselves to work, to do their shopping - or merely to ride for pleasure. This results from many factors, the most important being the high cost of transport, and the real need for more exercise.

| 1| 2| 3| 4| 5| 6| 7| 8| 9| 10| 11| 12|

NATIONAL BUILDING SOCIETY

National House
Sussex Road
Boston Lincs
PE17 4AG

Tel 27184

②

Ref EAJ/DB/1063

②

(Date)

②

Mrs B Winterbottom
2 East Avenue
ROCHESTER
Kent ME2 4PX

②

Dear Madam

①

I have heard from your former Branch which has refunded
the sum of £8.70 in respect of commission charged in
error.

①

... I enclose a Proposal Form for Property Bond Investment,
as you requested.

①

Yours faithfully

⑤

E Jameson
Manager

②

enc

Enclosure(s)   The text of a letter will usually say if
something is being enclosed, but this is not enough.
The word enclosure—or more often just enc, Enc or
ENC—should be typed at the foot of the letter. For more
than one enclosure, encs, Encs, or ENCS is used. Often
the number of enclosures is specified—enc 1, encs 2,
etc. The nature of the enclosure may be stated, eg enc
invoice. The form enc is the quickest and it is wise to
show the number of enclosures.

Marginal mark(s)   An alternative or addition is to
type three unspaced dots in the left-hand margin at
each point where there is reference to an enclosure. Use
the margin release to backspace into the left-hand
margin five times (allowing two spaces between the
last marginal mark and the left-hand margin position).
This sign is used to check that all enclosures are sent
with the letter.

Name of signatory   Often the name of the person
signing the letter is typed under the space left for the
signature (especially useful when the signature is
barely, if at all, legible!).

Official position of signatory   If included, this is
typed on the line following the name.

What is display?

'Display' in typewriting means good arrangement of the typed material on the page. In continuous typing this is usually just a matter of headings and good and consistent margins—at the top, bottom and sides of the paper. However, display work is of varying complexity and includes the layout of notices, menus, programmes, tables, and so on. But the basic requirement is always the same—good positioning of the typed material on the page.

It is important you realize that 'display' or 'layout' does not mean that everything has to be elaborately centred. Many expert typists often 'block' headings, columns, etc. However, there will be occasions when you will want to centre typed matter and you should know how to do it. (Electronic typewriters have an automatic centre facility.)

All displayed work requires skilful use of paper space and a feeling for pleasing and artistic arrangement. Display skill can be developed with practice—but it is necessary to select the right size of paper for a particular task and to understand 'paper scales' (how many letters/characters/spaces can be typed *across* a sheet of paper, and how many lines can be typed *down* a page).

Paper scales

1   Take a sheet of A4 paper and hold it with the shorter edge against the paper bail, with the left edge of the paper positioned against 0 on the paper bail scale. Move the paper grips out of the way when you do this.

2   Note the paper scale point at the right-hand edge of the paper. If your typewriter has elite pitch, it will be 100; with the larger pica pitch it will be 82. This means that you can type either 100 or 82 characters/spaces across a sheet of A4 paper—and the centre point of the paper would therefore be at 50 or 41 respectively.

3   Now use, in turn, a sheet of A4 and a sheet of A5 paper, to check the following figures:

Spaces across the page on	A4 portrait	A5 landscape	A5 portrait
Elite (12 to 2.5 cm or 1 in)	100	100	70
Pica (10 to 2.5 cm or 1 in)	82	82	58

To centre a single line on A5 landscape (with manual and electric typewriters)

Report on New Office Filing System
ᴗ ᴗ ᴗ ᴗ ᴗ ᴗ ᴗ ᴗᴗ ᴗ ᴗ ᴗ ᴗ ᴗᴗᴗ ᴗ
1 2 3 4 5 6 7 8 9 10 11 12 13 14 15 16 17

1   Insert a sheet of A5 paper (landscape) in your typewriter, making sure it is straight and the left-hand edge is at 0 on the paper scales.

2   Move the margin stops out of the way—to the extreme right and left positions.

3   Set the line-space selector at 1.

4   Adjust your paper (by turning the right-hand cylinder knob) so that its top edge is flush with the alignment scale.

5   Use the carriage return thirteen times.

6   Move your carriage (by using a carriage release lever) until the printing point is at the centre of the page (at 50 with elite; at 41 with pica).

7   Say each letter in the line to yourself and, as you do so, backspace once for every two characters (letters and spaces) in the heading. In this example there is one space between words: thus there are 34 characters, so you will backspace 17 times, as shown above. Here you have an even number of letters—but whenever an odd letter is left over, ignore it.

8   Now type the heading. Note there is no full stop after a heading.

Check the figures that follow.

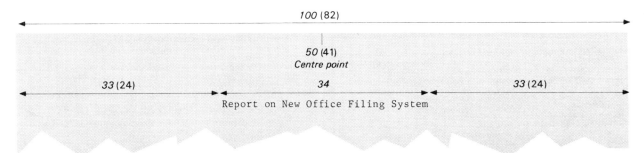

The zebra's very quaint stripes are just camouflage, an excellent blend with the background of tall grasses on the African plains.

1   *Technique Section 12C (page 59)*

Type the letter given in the Technique Section on A5 paper. Leave the indicated number of lines of space between the parts of the letter : these are shown by ringed figures.

Margins: elite—9 left, 64 right
              pica—7 left, 54 right

2   On A5 paper type the two following letters in the same style as in the last task, using the same margins. Remember to insert today's date. Take a carbon copy of **b**.

a

Ref ALJ. SJ

Mrs P Brown, 45 Acre Lane, SOUTHAMPTON, SO2 4JK

Dr Madam / I enclose a cheque recd from the National Building Society's Liverpool office for the amount of £98.76. This represents the 3 months' excess interest paid to the Society on the redemption of the mortgage on yr Liverpool property, which has now been sold.

Yrs truly

A L Jones   Manager   enc cheque

b

Your ref RW. ag. 1246
Our ref SP. kg

The Midlands Brick Co Ltd, 48 Fore Street, BIRMINGHAM, B6 3TA

Dear Sirs / The dry weather during the last 2 mths has enabled us to progress much faster than we had expected with our housing scheme in Kingslake Park. We shd therefore be very grateful if you wd advance yr schedule of brick deliveries by 3 weeks.

Yrs ffly s Picker Office Manager

SI 1.12

We all like to discuss television programmes. Some say that by and large they are a waste of time, but this is the wrong way to look at it. The truth is that there is something for all. We must each choose what suits us, and leave the rest.

| 1| 2| 3| 4| 5| 6| 7| 8| 9| 10| 11| 12|

Drill:
alphabetic paragraph

Biology is the science which deals jointly with animal and plant life. It includes zoology, which inquires into the variety and life ways of animals, and botany, which explores the plant kingdom.

1 *a* *Technique Section 12E* (*page 63*)

Type the letter in the Technique Section on an A4 printed letterhead and take a carbon copy.

Margins: elite—12 left, 90 right
           pica—10 left, 75 right

b *Technique Section 13* (*page 64*)

Type a **DL** envelope for the letter typed in the last task.

c Check again that your typing of the letter is mailable. (All your finished work should, of course, be mailable.)

d Then read through your carbon copy. Is it legible? Have any necessary corrections been carefully made on it?

e Fold the letter as shown in the diagram on page 64 and insert it in its envelope (ignore the lack of a signature and an enclosure for this purpose).

2 *a* Type the following letter on A4 headed paper, taking a carbon copy. Use the same style and margins as in task **1***a* above.

b Carry out the same procedures as in **1***b* to **1***e* above.

Southern Books Ltd
32 The Broadway
BOURNEMOUTH
Hants
BH10 4HT

FOR THE URGENT ATTENTION OF THE MANAGER

Dear Sirs

Further to yr telephone call of this morning, I am disappointed to know that the 2 most important books in my order are out of stock, although you expect to receive new supplies soon.

My need for these books is very urgent so I must ~~ask you~~ cancel my order for them and ask you to return my money. [I have checked with a large bookseller in London that they hold stocks of these books so I shall go there and purchase the books in person. [Kindly forward the other books I ordered from you.

as soon as possible

Yrs ffly

N Weston
Head of English Department

SI 1.16

S/A 25 (2 minutes)

I seldom go to London, but make the most of each visit. For a start I choose a good hotel near the West End. From there the theatres and the best shops are close at hand as well as the museums and art galleries. I ask for no more than this.

| | 1| 2| 3| 4| 5| 6| 7| 8| 9| 10| 11| 12|

Anglo American Travel Co

46 High Street · Oxford
Telephone: Oxford 4482

②

Ref DPS/BO

②

(Date)

②

Mr L Bruce
48 Drake Gardens
OXFORD
OX3 4BT

②

Dear Sir
①
HOLIDAY IN NEW ENGLAND
①
Further to our telephone conversation, I have pleasure
in enclosing an information brochure on the New England
States. Also enclosed is a booking form for the flight
provisionally reserved for you to travel from London to
New York on 20 August, returning 29 September.
①
Yours faithfully
ANGLO-AMERICAN TRAVEL CO

⑤

D Sharp
Assistant Manager

②

encs

Subject heading Often a business letter includes a key description of the subject at the head of the letter, after the salutation. With the fully-blocked style of layout, this is best typed in closed capital letters: initial capitals with underscoring can be used but it takes more time. A subject heading should not be followed by a full stop.

Name of firm after complimentary close Sometimes a business letter repeats, after the complimentary close, the name of the firm or organization sending the letter. This should be typed on the line following the complimentary close, in closed capitals.

The following diagram shows the most common IPS (International Paper Size) envelopes—and how to fold A4 and A5 paper to fit them. In business, the two most commonly used sizes of envelopes are:

C6—114 mm × 162 mm (approx $4\frac{1}{2}$ in × $6\frac{3}{8}$ in). Takes A4 folded twice, A5 folded once.
C5/6—110 mm × 222 mm (approx $4\frac{1}{4}$ in × $8\frac{5}{8}$ in). Takes A4 folded into three, A5 folded once.

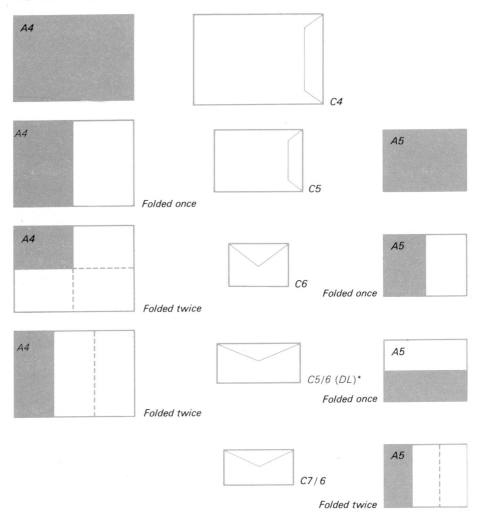

DL stands for 'DIN lange'. The standard and rational system of paper and envelope sizes now in general use (International Paper Sizes) was originally drawn up by the Deutsche Industrie Normen (DIN)—German Industry Standards. 'Lange' means long.

Banker envelopes   These have the flap along the longer side of the envelope (the last three envelopes shown above, for instance).

Pocket envelopes   These envelopes have their flap along the shorter side (as with the first two envelopes shown above).

Typewriter envelopes   Special typewriter envelopes are available in banker style. They have a narrow, straight-edged sealing flap that enables the typist to obtain a better finish to her work, since she does not have to type over an uneven surface.

Different qualities   As with correspondence paper, envelopes are available in a variety of paper qualities, eg bond, parchment, manila. Most business firms match the quality of their envelopes with their correspondence paper.

An abbey suffered a sorry fate but the killings were sadder.
Kindness and good manners really matter for a happy feeling.
The accident rate in the bigger towns in summer is horrific.

1 *Technique Section 12D (page 61)*

a Type the letter in the Technique Section on A5 paper and take a carbon copy.

Margins: elite—9 left, 64 right
pica—7 left, 54 right

b Type a DL envelope for the letter.

c After checking that the work is mailable, clip the papers together, ready for signature. (Carbon copy under top copy; flap of envelope folded over uppermost part of top copy—secured with a slip-on paper clip.)

2 Type the following letter on A5 paper, taking a carbon copy. Use the same style and margins as in task **1***a* above. Do not forget to insert today's date and indicate enclosures.
When you have finished typing, carefully check that the letter is of mailable standard. Then type a DL envelope for it and follow the same procedure as in **1***c* above.

R/ Ref #W. ew. 2734

Mrs B Crawford
26 East Lane
ANDOVER
SP8 6AJ

Dear Mrs Crawford

BUSINESS NEWS DIGEST

We are disappointed that although we have / written to you to *twice*
ask whether you wish us to continue sending your mthly
copy of Business News Digest, you have not replied to
our letters.

Please complete and return the enclosed ~~pre~~ reply-paid
card without delay.

Yrs sincerely
ACE PUBLICATIONS

R Waters
Circulation Supervisor

SI 1.19

A good secretary should have a feel and a love for language.
For this it helps just to read a lot of good books. Writing
of any sort trains the mind to choose apt words and phrases.
A good style grows with practice, and brings its own reward.

| 1 | 2 | 3 | 4 | 5 | 6 | 7 | 8 | 9 | 10 | 11 | 12 |

Attention line If a letter is addressed to an organization (in which case the salutation will be Dear Sirs) but the writer wants it to be dealt with by a particular person, this is indicated in one of the following styles. (This does not mean that the letter is personal, simply that the sender knows who will deal with it. By addressing the letter to the firm, it will still be opened if the person mentioned is away from the office.)

The attention line is often typed between the inside address and the salutation—**where it is clearly visible**.

Confidential, personal, urgent, etc These are typed in the same way as the attention line, and positioned between the date and the inside name and address.

Attention of Mr F Brownlow

Attention: Mr F Brownlow

For the Attention of Mr F Brownlow

FOR THE ATTENTION OF MR F BROWNLOW

---

②

(Date)

②

Nationwide Garage Chain Ltd
22-24 Fenton Way
SHEFFIELD
S7 9EF

①

FOR THE ATTENTION OF MR F BROWNLOW

①

Dear Sirs

①

You will no doubt be interested to know that a completely new edition of the MOTOR STATION MANUAL is now available. As you are probably aware, this manual has been recognized for many years as an authoritative guide for service station proprietors and executives, and for students and others contemplating a career in the motor trade.

①

... The enclosed copy of a press release indicates the broad coverage of the new manual which we are sure you would find valuable in your business. If you are already familiar with this work, you will appreciate the topics that have been added in this new edition.

①

The new MOTOR STATION MANUAL, fully up to date in every way, is priced at £9.50 (including postage and packing). However, we should be pleased to arrange for copies to be invoiced at £9 each for a minimum of 5 copies.

①

Yours truly

⑤

A Jackson
Circulation Manager